THINK OUTSIDE THE COUNTRY

A guide to going global
and succeeding in the
translation economy

John Yunker

Byte
Level
Books

Think Outside the Country: A Guide to Going Global
and Succeeding in the Translation Economy

Published by Byte Level Books

Ashland, Oregon

www.bytelevelbooks.com

© 2017 John Yunker

ISBN: 978-1-61822-049-3

Library of Congress Control Number: 2016919625

Contents

Welcome to the translation economy

On November 11, 2016, a visitor to Amazon's China website was greeted with a promotion for the Kindle with the numbers 11.11 featured prominently:

What's the big deal about *11.11*?

Amazon was celebrating Singles Day, a relatively new Chinese holiday and a product of the internet itself. A day when millions of young people celebrate being single—and do a little online shopping. Actually, *a lot* of online shopping.

Singles Day is now the busiest and richest day of online commerce on the planet. Nearly US$18 billion was spent on this day in 2016.

To put this in perspective, Black Friday (the day after Thanksgiving in the United States) generated just $3 billion. And Singles Day isn't just about buying electronic gadgets and clothing; a record 100,000 cars were sold in China on this day, also online.

American-based multinationals are acutely aware of Singles Day. Companies such as Costco, Procter & Gamble, and Nike prepare special website promotions, such as Nike in 2016:

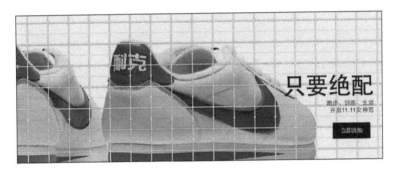

Nike now earns more than half of its revenues from outside the US, with China accounting for 11 percent. Apple, which also generates more than half of its revenues from outside the US, relies most heavily on China for its international revenues. Microsoft is also heavily invested in this market with its own 2016 Singles Day promotion:

Singles Day is just one day

Despite the significance of this ecommerce extravaganza, Singles Day is just one day in one country, in a world in which more and more companies are not selling only to one country but to ten or twenty or a hundred. Every country has its unique holidays and cultural traditions. Every country is a new frontier, a new opportunity for anyone with global aspirations.

Here's where things get interesting.

While companies generally focus on a few major markets, such as China and Germany, France and Japan—the smart companies keep their eyes open to *all* countries, because you never know where the next opportunity will arise.

Consider Facebook; its largest market, based on number of users, is India, followed by the US, Brazil, and Indonesia. And Twitter enjoys a higher percentage of users in countries such as Turkey, South Africa, and Japan than in its home market. This phenomenon is not unique to US companies. Take a look at this home page from an upstart Chinese mobile phone brand called Vivo. Note the countries displayed on the right:

Instead of targeting developed markets like Germany and the

US, Vivo is targeting emerging economies such as Indonesia, Vietnam, and Myanmar. And, once it gets its footing in these emerging markets, I won't be surprised to see more developed markets added to the list.

That's the world we live in today—one in which emerging markets are just as relevant as developed markets to companies that seek global success. The internet has connected the world's economy to such an extent that executives and their companies can no longer afford to ignore any country beyond their borders.

For those executives who keep their heads down, focused only on their home markets, this revolution has occurred largely unnoticed, taking place on those country websites that most of us will never visit. But I hope by the end of this book you will invest time to explore this fast-evolving multilingual internet. Because those of us who are more curious than intimidated by languages and cultures we may not understand are best positioned to succeed in this new translation economy.

The information economy is now the translation economy

The internet connected the world's computers, and the digitization of content enabled the rapid flow of information around the world, which drove several decades of what came to be known as the information economy. One of the great myths of the information economy—and the World Wide Web, for that matter—was this idea that a company could go global simply by launching a website.

True, your website might reach around the planet, but this doesn't ensure that people will use it. Information is useless if you don't understand it.

The information economy has for too many years exhibited an English-language bias. It wasn't very long ago when marketing executives would tell me they believed (or hoped) that the world would all speak English one day, making their lives so much easier. True, millions of people are learning English as a second language, but they're not necessarily purchasing in their second language. And there are a lot of languages out there besides English:

You can wait for the world to speak your language, or you can get busy speaking its languages. In other words, you can enter the *translation economy*.

At its most basic level, the translation economy is the globalization of the information economy. Think of it as a *linguistic and cultural interface* between you and everyone else around the world. This interface works in both directions. It translates what you have to say to the world and also translates the world back to you.

The translation economy is the natural evolution of a more interconnected planet, in which more than half the world's population, through their smartphones and computers, not only have internet access but the means and the will to purchase through it.

In the translation economy, companies must be fluent in many languages across many geographies. Every country, no matter how small, has the potential to add to your bottom line.

In the translation economy, translation is no longer an afterthought; it is a competitive advantage. Speed of translation. Quality of translation. Cultural relevance. All of these elements determine whether your mobile apps, websites, brand names, products and services, and, ultimately, your company will succeed in new markets.

In the translation economy, governments must create environments that encourage companies to expand globally and hire linguistically and culturally diverse employees. And for governments that create barriers to entry, companies must work to overcome these barriers.

In the translation economy, fewer people are marginalized simply because they don't speak your language. Languages are no longer the obstacles to education and commerce that they once were.

In the translation economy, translation is power
The phrase "lost in translation" may be a cliché, but it's one that is all too relevant. If you don't hire the right translators, what is getting lost in translation is your revenues. Companies use translation to keep an eye on their competitors, to monitor blogs, to monitor the media across any number of languages.

Computers are playing a larger role in helping companies translate content. Google could ultimately play the largest role of all.

Google Translate translates more than 100 billion words each day.

If you assume that a web page includes roughly 100 words, then we're talking about one billion web pages translated per day. Google doesn't break out the language numbers, but the fact that Google Translate now supports 100 languages (with more on the way) speaks to why this service is so popular. More than 500 million people use the service every day.

And yet there are more than 6,000 languages spoken in more than 200 countries. Google has a long way to go.

But we all do.

Most companies support fewer than 10 languages on their websites and mobile apps. Which means we're just getting started and, for those of us who embrace the necessary chaos of going global, the world provides limitless opportunities. As the translation economy evolves, we will see the breadth of languages and the depth of translated content expand dramatically.

Welcome to the translation economy.

The translation economy timeline

Globalization is often viewed as a contemporary trend, and yet the forces of globalization have been with us since before the Silk Road. Whenever two or more cultures trade goods or trade bullets, there is also an exchange of information and ideas. But until recently this transfer of information was relatively limited to a small number of people.

The *translation economy* is unique to our time in its reliance on the internet and mobile platforms to connect billions of people. Which is where companies and organizations like Microsoft, Google, Apple, Wikipedia, Facebook, and Snapchat have, in just a few decades, changed the world that we live in. Never before have so many people had access to so many other people across every country and culture on the planet.

From the Silk Road to Silicon Valley
I mark the beginning of the translation economy in 1996, when Yahoo!, the world's leading search engine at the time, first expanded into Japan.

From that moment on, here are notable developments over the past two decades:

1996   Yahoo! launches Yahoo! Japan, the first significant example of website localization.

1998   Amazon begins its global expansion, launching localized websites for Germany and the United Kingdom.

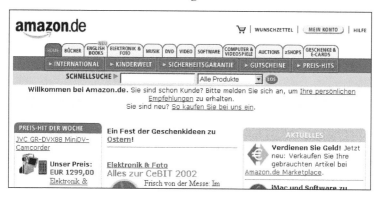

1999   Google, just a year old, begins recruiting volunteers to help translate its search engine interface.

2000   H&R Block becomes the first company to launch a Spanish-language website aimed specifically at the US Hispanic market.

2001   Wikipedia is born.

2002   Babel Fish is used by AOL and Alta Vista to provide users with free, real-time translation.

2002   Google offers its search interface in more than 60 languages.

2005   Google surpasses 100 languages.

2006   Google begins expanding the linguistic reach of Google Translate.

2007   Wikipedia offers content in more than 250 languages.

2008   Facebook relies on volunteer translators to launch its first localized site into Spanish.

2009   Google Translate reaches 41 languages.

2010   Facebook goes from 2 languages to more than 70 languages in 18 months.

2011   Mobile app localization goes mainstream.

2013   Google Translate supports 65 languages.

2014   Wikipedia surpasses 270 languages.

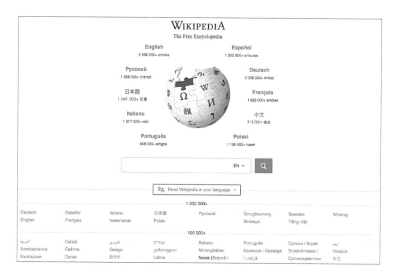

2015   Gmail supports 59 languages.

2015   Uber's mobile app supports 36 languages, more than the Uber website.

2016   Mobile messaging app Facebook Messenger is available in 29 languages; Snapchat and WeChat are available in 20 languages.

2016   Google Translate supports 103 languages, effectively addressing the language needs of 99% of all internet users.

Looking back over this timeline, it's hard to ignore the growth of languages and its direct impact on a company's success. Companies like Facebook and Google owe a great deal of their success to their early and aggressive investments in going global. What I find tragic are all the companies that have underestimated the value of going global over the years and have under-invested in it.

Why this book?

There is an assumption, widely held, that to succeed globally you must be some sort of global savant—one of those people who speaks a half-dozen languages, carries a passport bulging with extra pages, and was seemingly born in an international departure lounge.

The truth is that global success requires considerably fewer airline miles than you might think. Global success requires a simple desire to understand the world outside your own.

It's time to "opt in"

As I write these words, the United Kingdom has voted to exit the European Union, and the United States has elected a self-avowed nationalist intent on tearing up trade agreements. I empathize with those who fear globalization. Many corporations and governments have taken advantage of poorly constructed or poorly implemented trade deals, and people, animals, and environments have suffered greatly. But global trade, if practiced ethically and with empathy, can be a positive force. It connects us, it helps us to move beyond our differences, and it raises standards of living around the world.

Which is a big reason why I wrote this book—to demystify the differences between us. Yes, the world outside our borders can feel overwhelming at times. The sheer number of languages, cultural and religious practices, and the speed at which societies are evolving has resulted in people choosing to mentally *opt out* from the world at large.

This book is about *opting in*. And despite the strident words coming from the leadership of the UK and the US, nobody is suggesting the end of trading among countries, just doing so under different terms. People have been trading with one another since the beginning of civilization and will continue until the end of civilization.

Those who do opt out of the global economy will ultimately miss out. They will miss out on career opportunities and new learning opportunities, and they will miss out on the fascinating complexity of humanity.

Become a global generalist
I wrote this book to share what I've learned over nearly two decades, a journey that did not begin by learning a half-dozen languages. In fact, I'm fluent only in English, though I've invested much time in learning a little bit about a great many languages.

I've learned that you can be a language and cultural *generalist* and be quite successful in helping companies, websites, and products go global.

This book isn't strictly about taking a website or mobile app global, though you'll find plenty of real-world examples about how to do just that. Ultimately, this book is about taking *yourself* global. It's about providing an understanding of the globalization process along with country and cultural insights so you know what questions to ask when you're asked to, say, introduce a product into a new market or launch a global marketing campaign.

This book is intended for people who want to help their organizations expand into new markets as efficiently as possible without any embarrassing or costly mistakes. And this book is about showing respect for the people who live in these markets.

You won't speak every language, understand every culture. And that's okay. Nobody knows everything. There are plenty of polyglots and self-proclaimed global experts out there who appear to know everything.

Trust me, they don't.

But we can all know a little bit about a lot. More important, we can know what questions to ask. This book is about learning what we don't know as much as learning what we do know.

It's a big world out there. Nobody understands all of it. And that's what makes this all so exciting.

NEW RULES OF THE TRANSLATION ECONOMY

While the information economy was propelled by creators of content, the translation economy is propelled by translators of content. Here are six rules to keep in mind as you navigate this new world.

The internet connects computers; language connects people

Just because people in France and Brazil and Japan can view your website does not mean they can understand it, let alone purchase from it.

You would think this would be obvious to the leaders of the world's largest companies, and yet they live in a very different world than the rest of us. When the CEO of a company in one country visits the CEO of a company in another country, the odds are good that English is the common language. Over time, it's natural for executives to assume that there is a high degree of English fluency around the world; after all, if their counterparts speak and understand English, wouldn't the rest of their employees and customers as well? Actually, no.

English is the world's *second* language

Despite the high rates of English instruction around the world, the fact is that most people are not fluent in English and probably never will be, just as millions of Americans study a few years of a second language but will never be fluent in that second language. English may be the world's *lingua franca*, but it will always be a second language for most people. Native languages are what matter most; the following graph illustrates the native languages spoken by the 3.4 billion internet users today.

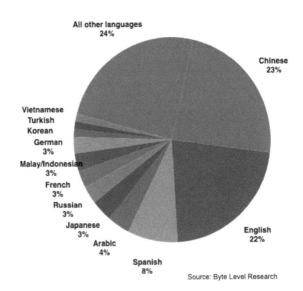

**Languages spoken by
the world's 3.4 billion internet users**

All other languages
24%

Chinese
23%

Vietnamese
Turkish
Korean
German
3%

Malay/Indonesian
3%

French
3%

Russian
3%

Japanese
3%

Arabic
4%

Spanish
8%

English
22%

Source: Byte Level Research

Chinese is now the dominant online language, followed by English and Spanish. But even if you support the ten largest language slices, you will still miss out on reaching vast numbers of internet users. The largest slice of this pie represents *all other languages*. This slice includes more than a hundred languages, such as Italian, Dutch, Swedish, Hindi, and Tamil. This slice will continue to expand as the next billion internet users come online over the next decade. And the English slice of the pie will continue to shrink.

That's not to say that your English-language website will become any less important on the internet; English is considered the default language for any company launching a global website. However, companies that hope to succeed globally will need to continue adding and expanding their non-English websites.

Speaking in tongues: the multilingual internet

The internet, like a mirror, reflects the people who use it, create content for it, and make purchases through it. And as more people come online, this mirror will reflect the world's many languages.

The most common question executives ask when going global is what languages they must support. Translation isn't cheap, nor is it a static resource that you pay for once and forget about. As your source (English) text changes, so too must your target language text. And if you're creating and updating text on a daily basis, as most companies do, your translation costs could be significant.

Because language is a means to an end, the smartest way to develop a language strategy is to work back from your target audience. If you intend to succeed in mainland China, Germany, France, and Italy, you will need to support Simplified Chinese,

German, French, and Italian. And as you broaden your global aspirations, so too will you broaden your language portfolio. And the safe bet is that you will continue to add languages over the years. Consider the following language totals from these companies from 2004 to 2017:

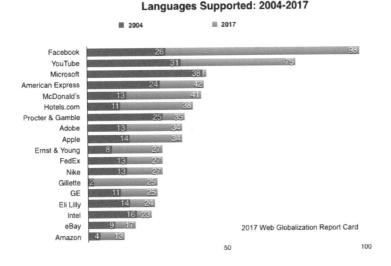

Languages Supported: 2004-2017

■ 2004   ■ 2017

2017 Web Globalization Report Card

Companies such as Facebook, FedEx, Adobe, and Apple have all doubled the number of languages they support over the past decade.

The majority of people who use the internet today are not native-English speakers. As their buying power improves—which it surely will—companies and their competitors will begin speaking to these new internet users in their native languages.

If you don't translate it, your customers will

What's the most popular translation tool in the world?

You've probably already used it: Google Translate. This tool has come a long way over the past decade; here is a view of what Google Translate looked like back in 2006, when Chinese, Japanese, and Korean were still BETA languages.

Over the years, Google Translate has continually added languages, as illustrated below:

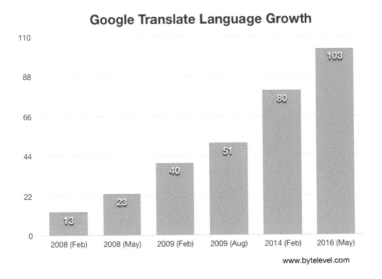

Google Translate Language Growth

Google Translate today supports more than 100 languages, reaching more than 99% of all internet users.

To get an idea of just how popular Google Translate has become, consider the following data points from 2016:

- 100 billion words translated per day
- 500 million users around the world
- Most common translations are between English and Spanish, Arabic, Russian, Portuguese, and Indonesian
- Brazilians are the heaviest users of Google Translate

Machine translation democratizes languages

Google Translate is known as a machine translation engine. The term carries over from decades earlier, when computers were known as machines; this should give you an idea of just how long engineers have been trying to create computers that could translate human languages.

In 2006, the quality of Google Translate was so poor that many translators believed the service would never replace human translators. Today, Google Translate is good enough for people to get the gist of what the content means, though it still isn't close to replacing human translators. Companies rely on professionals to translate their user manuals, websites, and software.

But for the rest of us, Google Translate will suffice. Besides, there are not nearly enough professional translators to translate 100 billion words per day. Nor is the average web user going to pay a professional to translate the home page of a foreign website. This is where Google Translate fits in quite nicely. And the odds are quite good that people are using Google Translate right now to translate your website into their language.

Good enough wins over perfect

The success of Google Translate illustrates that we will readily accept poor to average translations versus no translations at all. Google Translate has taken translation "to the people." It has opened doors and eyes and raised language expectations around the world. So it's not surprising that a number of large companies are now using machine translation, some translating several billion words per month. Companies such as Intel, Autodesk (shown below), and Adobe now allow customers to self-translate certain web pages.

Many more companies are certain to follow. Either you translate your website, or your customers will do it for you.

The internet has many borders

You'd think that a borderless internet would lead to a more borderless world. But actually the opposite has occurred. The internet may be technically borderless, but a growing number of countries are creating virtual and legal borders. Even navigating from a global website to a country website, as shown below on the Eli Lilly site, feels a little like passing through customs:

But small disclaimers are just the tip of the iceberg as the virtual world becomes more like our physical world, and this will create ongoing challenges and opportunities.

The rise of the *splinternet*
In late 2016, Russia blocked LinkedIn because the company did not store its citizen information on databases located within the country. This development is not unique to Russia. Germany also wants American companies to keep its citizens' information behind German borders. Brazil is following a similar trajectory. As more countries pursue these strategies, the internet will increasingly be known as the *splinternet*.

And then there is China, home of the Great Firewall, a term for its massive internet filtering and censorship efforts. For years, China has blocked companies such as Facebook and Twitter because the companies don't (yet) allow China to censor content. China's firewall encourages companies to register for licenses to host their websites within the country and play by China's rules. Hopefully, China will remain an extreme case study of virtual border control.

As you think about your global strategy, always keep in mind that borders can be just as real on the internet as they are in life, even if these borders show themselves through cookie opt-in forms, which are driven by EU regulations:

Borders happen. Plan accordingly.

People don't buy from global companies

Do you buy coffee from Starbucks because it has more than 25,000 stores in 70 countries? Because it is opening one new store every day in China?

Or do you buy from Starbucks because it has a store around the corner from your office?

Globally successful companies get to be that way by succeeding locally. And by not assuming that success in one country guarantees success in other countries. No matter how global your company may be, every new country provides a new opportunity to succeed, or to fail.

In 2015, Walmart earned more than $130 billion from outside the US, in countries such as Canada, Mexico, China, and Japan. But global expansion has not come easily. Walmart failed in Germany and struggled mightily in Japan. *The New York Times* reported that its South Korea stores shelved products so high that customers needed ladders to reach them. And the company reportedly tried to sell ice skates in Mexico and golf clubs in Brazil, where the sport is not popular. Walmart has learned over the years, often the hard way, how to localize its stores and offerings to better accommodate customer needs and customs.

Also in 2015, Target retreated from Canada, a country just a few hundred miles north of its US headquarters. A country that cost the retailer more than a billion dollars in lost investments as well as the job of its CEO. The retail industry is perhaps the most difficult industry to take global because it is so complex, so competitive, so personal.

On the internet, place matters more, not less
Just because the internet has brought every brand and company to within reach doesn't mean that place no longer matters. If anything, customers are more sensitive to place than ever before.

We think geographically. We are partial to our *home team* businesses. *Made in America* isn't just a slogan, it's a deeply personal belief.

In the late 1990s, Japan was seemingly poised to take over the world. Honda and Toyota were "stealing" American jobs. What did these two companies do to assuage American sentiment? They began building cars in America, relying on American workers. And they made sure that everyone knew about it.

Americans aren't the only ones who like to purchase from local companies. If you're selling physical goods, you can be sure that your potential customers want to know where you're located. They want to know if they can return their purchase without having to pay international shipping fees. They want to know that they can get customer support in their language and in their time zone.

The "global" website that corporate communications departments create typically means little to the customer. It's a useful website for journalists who need fact sheets on the company or competitors, or for job seekers. But the people who actually wish to buy a product or service want to see your *local* website—something in their language supporting their currency.

Sometimes the place of origin is part of your brand. The European Union strictly enforces the protection of foods and beverages from specific regions, such as Gorgonzola and Feta, Bordeaux and Champagne. In the US, Napa Valley wines and Kentucky Bourbon are also legally protected. Where the product comes from says something important about its quality. That's why there is so much emphasis today on protecting place names with truth in labeling.

It's not easy to succeed in "foreign" markets

Sometimes a simple change in worldview can go a long way in helping companies go global. I've found that companies that use the word *foreign* to describe the world outside their borders are often less equipped to succeed outside their borders.

The word itself feels as if you're assuming a given market is too different than your own to succeed within. Try *international* instead. Or focus on specific regions of the world.

A simple change in worldview can go a long way. Instead of thinking of your company as, say, an American company that sells to foreign markets, think of yourself as a global company that sells to local markets.

The sooner *foreign* markets become *local* markets, the closer you'll be to succeeding in these local markets.

There is no such thing as "rest of world"

It is common within most global companies to organize the world into three main categories:

1. Core markets

2. Emerging markets

3. Rest of world (ROW) markets

Core markets are where a company makes the most of its revenues, where it is most established. Emerging markets tend to be those countries with promising growth potential, such as China and India, where companies are investing for the long term.

Rest of world includes all those countries and regions that companies don't have the time or energy or resources to target. At least not yet. A company may have four or five core markets and a dozen emerging markets, with the remaining 150+ countries labeled as ROW.

In reality, there really is no such thing as rest of world. Every country is important. A country of just 3 million people could be very profitable. And, collectively, all these ROW countries add up to more than a billion people. Companies that diversify their global strategies to include a mix of emerging *and* developed markets position themselves for long-term success.

The best way to view ROW countries is as a temporary grouping, one that will fade away as your organization invests in all markets outside of your domestic market. This may be a very long way away, but it's important to keep this goal in mind. Many executives I work with at one point believed they would only need to support a dozen or so localized websites, only to realize, years later, that this number exceeded 50 or more.

By viewing every country and culture on equal terms, you will maintain a better degree of respect and support for all customers —present and future.

Global generalists create global companies

Think globally; act locally. It's a catchy slogan.

In practice, however, I find the opposite to be true. We act *locally* and, with great effort, think *globally*.

It's not easy to think globally, at least not in the literal sense of the word. Does any one person fully understand the thousands of languages and cultures and sub-cultures around the world? When you create a new product or website can you easily imagine how it will be used by people in Kenya, Saudi Arabia, Argentina, Japan, and Pakistan, to name just a few?

When we develop a new product, a new website, or new page of text we generally picture a target audience broadly in line with ourselves—people who speak the same language, share a similar culture, perhaps live in the same country. This is only natural. It's difficult—if not impossible—to write or create something for an audience you don't understand.

And we can't understand everyone, can we?

Consider the plight of the *global* marketing executive, an individual tasked with marketing to the world. An individual expected to understand the world and all its opportunities and pitfalls.

How does this executive manage so many countries and cultures without going crazy? By becoming a *global generalist*.

As in medicine, a general practitioner knows the entire body but also knows when to call in the specialist. To succeed globally, every company needs at least one global generalist, preferably many.

Why you should become a global generalist

While you can't literally think globally, you *can* be a global generalist—someone who knows a little about a great number of countries and cultures and languages. By focusing on amassing a broad stretch of knowledge, you will be better prepared to ask the right questions about any new product or marketing initiative before taking it global.

Think of yourself as a global Swiss Army knife, one that has developed a diverse set of skills attuned to the challenges of going global.

For example, if you understand the meaning of specific colors and numbers across Asian countries, you'll know that a product with the number 4 in its name is probably not a good idea (as this number, when spoken, sounds like the word "death" in countries such as China and Japan).

And by knowing this detail you can then be sure you ask similar questions about other markets. And, no, you don't have to quit your job and spend the next six months backpacking around the world, though you can certainly propose a sabbatical to your boss.

The best global executives are those who aren't afraid of saying "I don't know." Who aren't afraid to ask questions and to rely on cultural and linguistic experts to help guide them. The globalization of any product and business is by nature a team effort. And global generalists are best positioned to lead their organization to global success.

And now let's get started thinking globally.

THINK GLOBALLY

Nearly half of the world's population is now connected to the internet. Who are they, where are they, and how will you reach them?

If the world were 100 people

We share this planet with 7.4 billion other people across more than 200 countries speaking more than 6,000 languages.

These large numbers can be difficult to visualize. So let's instead look at the world by representing all 7.4 billion people as just 100 people. For starters, here's where we all live:

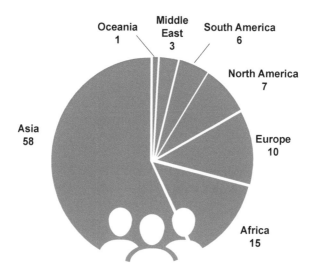

As you can see, more than half of the world's population lives in Asia, due largely to China and India, the two most-populous countries on the planet, with more than one billion people within each. And let's not overlook Indonesia, with more than 230 million people.

Africa accounts for 15 residents, which is significant when compared with Europe, which accounts for a paltry 10 residents. And North America accounts for just 7 of the world's 100 figurative people. You can be a very successful company selling to these 7 people, but you won't be a *globally* successful company until you learn how to sell to all 100.

Looking at global growth trends, it's safe to say that Asia is likely to gain a few residents in the years ahead, while Europe will continue to lose residents. So a good percentage of this book will address how companies are marketing themselves to residents of Asia. This is, after, where the people are.

But just because more than half of the world lives in Asia doesn't mean you can reach them with your website. Many still don't have internet access.

Just 49 people have internet access
More than 3.6 billion people currently have internet access (including those who access the internet through their smartphones). This number, while significant, still only accounts for about half the world's population.

Only 9 people speak English

Now here is where things get interesting. Of the 49 people with internet access, only nine people would be considered native-English speakers, as outlined here:

- 10 speak Chinese
- 9 speak English
- 4 speak Spanish
- 3 speak Portuguese
- 2 speak Arabic
- 1 speaks Japanese
- 1 speaks Russian
- 1 speaks Indonesian
- 1 speaks German
- 1 speaks French
- 16 speak *other* languages

These numbers are among the most challenging to calculate because millions of people are fluent in more than one language. But the key here is to focus on the diversity of languages represented by the world's internet users. And as for those 16 people who speak *other* languages, we're talking about 250 *other* languages, including Dutch, Swedish, Turkish, Korean, and Persian, to name just a handful. The most successful global websites also happen to be the most multilingual.

Websites speaking in tongues

Each year, for the past 15 years, I've reviewed the websites of more than 200 leading global companies. I track language use, navigation techniques, design, and global consistency. This data forms the basis for *The Web Globalization Report Card*, in which I benchmark these websites according to how well they present themselves to the world. As you can see below, the average number of languages supported by these global sites has doubled over the past decade.

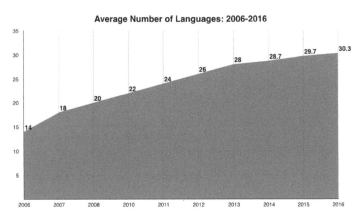

Average Number of Languages: 2006-2016

Source: Byte Level Research   2016 Web Globalization Report Card

Another year, another language

If there has been one consistent trend in web globalization over the past few years, it has been the steady diversification of languages. Some companies have experienced sudden spikes in the number of languages they support, such as Facebook, Visa, and Dyson, as shown here:

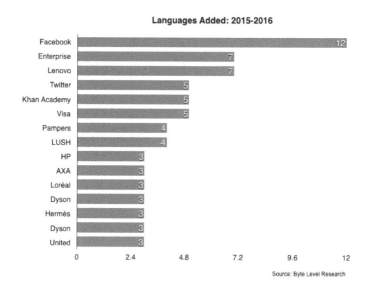

Languages Added: 2015-2016

Company	Languages Added
Facebook	12
Enterprise	7
Lenovo	7
Twitter	5
Khan Academy	5
Visa	5
Pampers	4
LUSH	4
HP	3
AXA	3
Loréal	3
Dyson	3
Hermès	3
Dyson	3
United	3

Source: Byte Level Research

For any globally oriented company, language growth is an inevitability. The degree of growth often reflects where a given company stands in the *language growth curve*. This curve begins rather steeply, as companies ramp up quickly in the core European and Asian languages. After a company reaches 20 languages, the curve begins to taper off. Most companies are still in the early stages of this growth curve. And what companies are at the outer reaches of this growth curve?

The language leaders

Here are the websites that lead in languages supported:

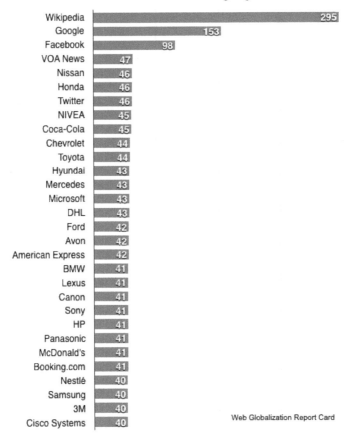

Leaders in Languages: 2017

Wikipedia	295
Google	153
Facebook	98
VOA News	47
Nissan	46
Honda	46
Twitter	46
NIVEA	45
Coca-Cola	45
Chevrolet	44
Toyota	44
Hyundai	43
Mercedes	43
Microsoft	43
DHL	43
Ford	42
Avon	42
American Express	42
BMW	41
Lexus	41
Canon	41
Sony	41
HP	41
Panasonic	41
McDonald's	41
Booking.com	41
Nestlé	40
Samsung	40
3M	40
Cisco Systems	40

Web Globalization Report Card

Wikipedia, at 295 languages, is arguably the world's most global website and proof of just how global a website can become when you have a passionate group of content contributors. After Wikipedia and Google, the number of languages supported by companies drops quickly. But most websites top out (for now) at about 40 languages, not including English. This breadth of languages gives a websites a reach of roughly 90% of all web users.

What languages should you support?

Naturally, your language portfolio should reflect your global growth strategy. But to give you an idea of which languages are generally considered global languages, here are the nine languages shared by the leading global websites:

- English

- Chinese (Simplified)

- French

- German

- Japanese

- Spanish (Latin American)

- Portuguese (Brazilian)

- Russian

- Italian

- Korean

Why is this list important? Because it means that web users around the world have become accustomed to seeing these languages supported, which probably means you should too.

Thinking beyond .com

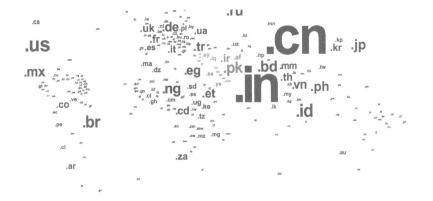

In the United States, the .com domain is viewed as both global and local, which, for the seven billion people who live outside of the United States, is a problem. Most global web executives tell me that between 50% and 80% of the visitors to their .com domains originate from outside the US, and millions of these visitors don't speak English. But because Americans and other native-English speakers are also visiting this same domain, companies struggle to serve very different visitors with very different needs. Which is why country codes (shown above) are enormously popular *outside* of the United States.

Canadians prefer .ca to .com, Australians prefer .au, and so forth. More than two-thirds of the world's largest brands now use country codes as the "front door" to at least some of their localized websites. Doing so has helped them improve their performance in search engines and, more important, has helped them appear more *local* to users.

A handful of companies, such as Amazon and Expedia, have gone a step further and incorporated these country code top-level domains (ccTLDs) into their logos, subtly localizing their brands.

Even if you can't acquire all country codes for all markets, make the most of the country codes you do have.

Internationalized Domain Names (IDNs)

When you want to visit Philips, you type www.philips.com into your web browser. Simple.

Now let's assume that you're French and you want to visit Philips France. In this case you would type www.philips.fr.

But now let's assume that you are Chinese and you want to visit the Philips China website.

The address is www.philips.cn.

For someone who speaks English, this address makes sense. But what about the native-Chinese speaker?

Here is the home page of Philips China—devoid of any Latin characters.

So if the website is in Chinese, why isn't the domain name also in Chinese? Because the internet was not designed to be multilingual. Support for non-Latin scripts has taken many years to evolve (and is not widely supported by many global brands).

But this is changing. Though it is not well promoted, Philips now supports a Chinese-language address for its China site:

www.飞利浦.中国

What you see here is the Chinese equivalent of *Philips* after www and the Chinese equivalent of *cn* to the far right.

Philips went one step forward and create a Chinese top-level domain for its brand name, shown here:

.飞利浦

While this domain is not yet functional, it is a sign of things to come—as in brand TLDs.

Dot.Brand

Since 2013, more than a thousand new top-level domains have been applied for—including many company brand names, known as brand TLDs. To give you a sense of the range of domains at play, here is a selected list:

.Ford
.Hermes
.Honeywell
.KPMG
.Merck
.Visa
.삼성 (Samsung)
.大众汽车 (Volkswagen)
. グーグル (Google)
.ストア (Translates to *Store*; owned by Amazon)

These new domains offer brands the potential benefits of higher search engine rankings and global marketing efficiencies.

And companies could also use their domains as truly global domains, instead of .com. FAGE is doing just that, using its brand domain with geographic subdomains for country websites, such as usa.fage for its US site page and deutschland.fage for its German site; unfortunately, it's not using the more standard .us and .de country codes.

Country codes, IDNs, and brand TLDs are addresses intended to help people find your websites more quickly. But there are other tools that companies employ to help users find their local websites, which come together in what I call the global gateway.

I'll cover the global gateway in the next section, Think Locally.

How to take anything global

Whether your goal is to take a website, product, or mobile app global there is a proven process for doing so effectively, a process fine-tuned over many years of trial and error. A process that includes two essential stages: *internationalization* and *localization*.

Internationalization   **Localization**

| Developing a *world-ready* product | Adapting the product for locales (languages, regions, cultures) |

Globalization = Internationalization + Localization

Internationalization is the process of modifying the product (or website, app, etc.) so that it can be adapted for any country, territory, or market with minimal re-engineering work. Localization is the process of modifying a product for a specific locale, which may be a country, a region, or some uniquely segmented demographic.

Internationalization and localization complement one another. The better job you do of internationalizing your product, the fewer problems you'll have when localizing your product for each market.

Internationalization

To best understand internationalization, think about how car companies build and sell cars. Not since the Model T have car makers offered just one model in one color. Today, you can get the Toyota Camry loaded with hundreds of different options. Each of these options may be viewed as *local* features, often unique to a given country or region.

Now imagine the complexity of supporting hundreds of local features across a hundred countries. And that's just one model of car, one of many. What if a car company could develop a global automotive platform, one that could be used not only to support all the various local features of that one model, but also be used across multiple car models?

That's internationalization, the process of creating a "world ready" product, one that can be efficiently localized for any market.

Like this world-ready global platform, courtesy of Toyota:

What you see here is not just an automotive frame but the result of the decades-long pursuit by Toyota to develop a global platform that can be used underneath a range of automobile brands.

Think about the challenges Toyota faced. It had to build a platform that could support a steering wheel on either side of the car, support front-wheel drive or rear-wheel drive, and support a range of body moldings, national and regional regulatory requirements, and customer-specific customizations.

Why go to so much trouble?

Because this global platform will save Toyota billions of dollars over the years ahead. Internationalization enables companies to be more efficient on a global scale. It's why Facebook uses one global design template across its 88 languages. It's why Uber offers one mobile app that supports 41 languages instead of 41 separate apps.

Some of the questions you'll ask during the internationalization phase include:

- *How global do we want to be?* How many countries and regions do you plan to target over the next three, five, ten years? These goals will determine how global your product platforms and website templates need to be.

- *How simple can we make the global platform or template so it can be shared globally?* Note that what you leave out of the design is just as important as what you include.

- *For any marketing, web, and product documentation, is the text "word ready"?* That is, can it be easily translated into all target languages, or does it include a lot of Americanisms, such as references to baseball?

- *What are the legal and regulatory requirements we must support across all of our target markets?*

- *For website and mobile apps, have we planned for regions that have slower data networks, where people are more sensitive to data consumption?*

Localization

Localization is a term that originated with the software industry. When software (or now a website or mobile app) is adapted to new markets, it is localized—a process that includes both technical and linguistic modifications.

While internationalization often happens behinds the scenes, localization is fully visible. The localization process includes making technical, visual, and textual modifications to your product.

Localization is all of these different-colored Toyota cars:

Questions you'll need to ask may include:

- *How do we localize our product mix?* For example, a retailer in Australia is selling winter clothes when North American retailers are selling summer clothes.

- *Are the visuals locally and culturally relevant?* The models you use, the clothing they wear, and the locations photographed all could be localized. Also, are your icons meaningful across all target users?

- *Are we compliant?* You must adapt to national and regional regulatory requirements.

- *Are we ecommerce friendly?* Supporting the local currency and payment methods is obvious, but not always easy to accomplish. Germans, for example, often prefer to pay by bank transfer over using credit cards.

- *Are we speaking their language?* Even countries that share a language may require translation, such as adapting a US website for the UK.

So now that you know what you need to do to take a product global, the good news is that you don't have to do everything on your own. There are many vendors who are able and eager to help you along the way.

You say translation agency; they say language service provider
Not very long ago, there were translation agencies and nothing more. These were businesses usually run by translators who translated whatever documents you sent them. But in the translation economy, even the word *translation* is up for debate. Many of the world's largest translation agencies now refer to themselves as Language Service Providers (LSPs).

Why is this? It's because agencies do a great deal more than translation these days. They provide interpretation services, video localization, software localization, testing, and search engine optimization across any language. They'll help you create consumer surveys and test your products in any market. They can be the eyes and ears of your consumers around the world.

An LSP may also be known as an SLV or MLV—which stands for single language vendor or multi-language vendor. These terms differentiate between vendors that handle only one language pair (such as a freelance translator) and larger vendors that handle any number of language pairs.

The mix of vendors you select will depend upon your industry, the types of products you need internationalized and/or localized, and the volume of work. It's common for the world's largest companies to work with multiple MLVs.

Translation in the cloud

Today, you're most likely to manage your translation vendors via a cloud-based service. These services allow for faster turnaround and integration with content management software. Long gone are the days of translators and project managers emailing files back and forth.

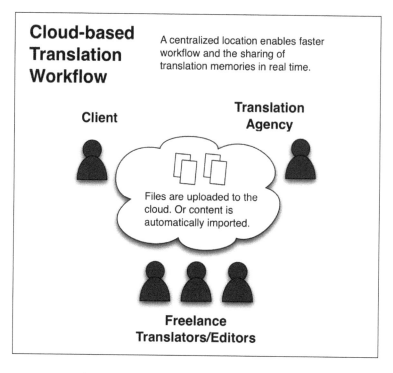

Cloud-based Translation Workflow

A centralized location enables faster workflow and the sharing of translation memories in real time.

Client

Translation Agency

Files are uploaded to the cloud. Or content is automatically imported.

Freelance Translators/Editors

Large LSPs that provide cloud-based platforms include Lionbridge, SDL, and Welocalize. There are also a growing number of cloud-based software platforms that allow you to select your own translator networks; companies include Smartling, Motionpoint, Transifex, OneSky, Tethras, Reverbeo, and Dakwak.

What's it going to cost?

Translation can cost from 5 cents per word to upwards of 30 cents per word. If you've got hundred of thousands of words to translate into dozens of languages, you're looking at a significant expense.

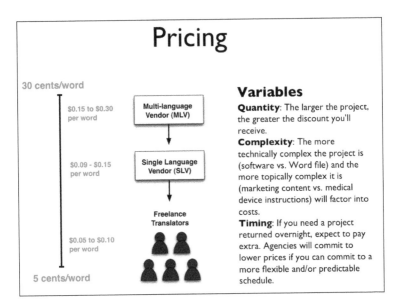

Costs are the reason why so much content remains untranslated. Companies either don't have the money or refuse to spend the money.

i18n and L10n

If you happen to come across these odd-looking abbreviations (known as numeronyms) you can blame software developers. The numbers refer to the number of letters between the first and last letters of the word, as in internationalization (i18n), localization (L10n), and globalization (g10n). These numeronyms are another reason why the globalization industry can be intimidating to outsiders. For more information on navigating the world of LSPs, check out my book *The Savvy Client's Guide to Translation Agencies.*

As you begin working with LSPs, don't be afraid to ask questions you might think are stupid. These companies often have decades of experience helping hundreds of companies go global and are often eager to help you avoid the mistakes of others that have gone before. The best vendors will become your partners around the world.

Conflicting names

Creating a global brand name is not easy, nor cheap. Not only do you need to test the name across all potential markets for trademark conflicts but you also need to test how that name will be perceived in each market. In 2016, Disney launched its new animated film *Moana*.

It's now common for Hollywood studios to launch films as simultaneously as possible in all countries to get ahead of the inevitable black market of pirated films. But in the rush to launch globally it seems that Disney overlooked a naming issue in Italy, in which Moana also happens to be the name of a well-known porn star.

Needless to say, the movie title was changed to *Oceania* in Italy.

Trademark conflicts also created obstacles. In other European markets, the film is called *Vaiana*, such as in Germany:

Transliteration of brand names

Taking a brand name global is difficult enough with Latin-based languages, but it becomes particularly challenging when going from English to, say, Russian or Japanese or Chinese. This is where transliteration comes in. Transliteration is the process of translating from one script to another; however, it does not translate the meaning.

For example, when Coca-Cola first entered the Chinese market, the company transliterated its brand name to Chinese characters, but the resulting name had no real meaning to consumers. That is, it sounded like Coca-Cola, but what does this word mean to people who have never heard it before?

After a period of slow sales, the company took another attempt at the name, creating a brand name that both sounded like the English-language name but also conveyed a positive meaning to Chinese consumers. Coca Cola (可口可乐) is translated as *delicious happiness.*

That's not to say that Coca-Cola doesn't use its Latin-based name in China. This too is commonly used on advertisements in the country as the company walks the fine line between being locally relevant while also carrying the cachet of an import.

However, the longer-term trend is toward embracing Chinese-specific brand names. Accor Brands now markets its Grand Mercure hotel brand within China as Mei Jue (美爵).

Local-by-design names
Sometimes it makes more sense to start from scratch in a new market, with a new brand name that is ideally suited to that market.

The InterContinental Hotels Group recently created a new hotel brand specific to China: Hualuxe, which, in English, loosely translates to *China luxury*.

Just "don't do it"

Slogans are also notoriously difficult to take global. Nike tried to translate its *Just Do It* slogan into other languages, but ultimately left the slogan in English. And, today, most local websites use no slogan at all. Notice that many of the leading global brands today, like Facebook, Google, and Starbucks, use no slogan whatsoever. As you plan your global marketing campaigns, you'd be wise to avoid trying to create a global slogan.

English-language brand names

Even English can be a challenge. When VW planned its new large SUV, it planned to use the name *Teramont* but dropped it after negative feedback from its US dealers. The dealers felt the name was too difficult to pronounce so VW went with a different name: Atlas.

When going global, be flexible

When we travel to different countries, we must adapt ourselves to different laws, customs, currencies, and the myriad unspoken social practices that define a culture. If you've traveled widely, you know that it's important to be flexible with your schedule, your plans, and your attitude, because nothing goes exactly as planned. Just as we must be flexible when we travel abroad, a website must be similarly flexible. The layout must adapt to different scripts and languages, and the content must adapt to different countries and cultures.

Text expansion (or contraction) happens

When text is translated, it doesn't stay the same length. The concept of *text expansion* occurs most often when translating from English into other languages, resulting in text that may expand by 30% to 50% or, in the case of Chinese, may contract. Consider the translation of the word *Search*:

Language	*Text*
English	Search
Chinese (Simplified):	搜索

Danish:	Søg
German:	Suche
French:	Rechercher

Text expansion or contraction can have a significant impact on the page counts of your printed catalogs, but why should you be concerned about text expansion on a web page? Because websites and software are often designed with English in mind, with very tight parameters. If not enough room is built into the design for text expansion or contraction, there will be problems.

The user interface is where expansion is most noticeable and, potentially, most troublesome. Compare the home page for Facebook in English:

And now in German:

Notice how the line of text above the user name input window stretches nearly across to the next window. Also notice how the text under the logo is a smaller type size to allow for more text.

Fortunately, Facebook's website is almost entirely text based, which means it is easy to tweak font sizes as needed for each localized website.

When translating into Asian scripts, because of the narrow strokes of the characters, fonts are often increased a point or two to improve legibility. Once again, a text-based, flexible design allows for give and take as you translate your website or software into another language.

Crossing the mobile divide

The science fiction writer William Gibson is credited with saying, "The future has arrived—it's just not evenly distributed yet."

The internet is very much like the future. It may touch all parts of the globe but not equally, such as with wireless networks. Network speeds vary dramatically across developed and emerging markets. Just because your Indonesian customer has a smartphone does not mean he or she has a blazing-fast 4G connection. In most markets around the world, slower 3G networks still dominate.

When going global, think slow

As in *slow wireless network*. The difference in user experience between a 3G and a 4G connection can be significant—particularly if your website was developed with a 4G network in mind. A mobile website can be localized into a hundred languages and still fail if mobile users don't have the patience to wait for it to display on their smartphones. Based on my research, many global websites have been developed with the assumption that mobile users around the world largely have 4G wireless connections.

Website weight and mobile performance

The fewer bits your website requires, the faster it will display (all other factors being equal) on the user's smartphone. Three seconds is widely considered a threshold above which consumers will lose patience on waiting for a website to load. If you have a 4G connection, more than half of the mobile websites listed below will display in less than three seconds.

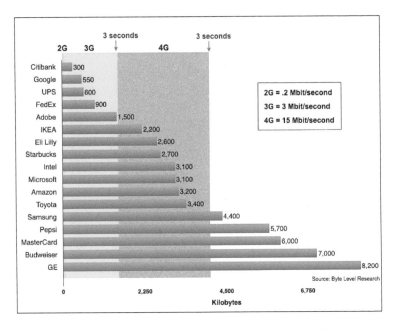

But if you have a 3G connection, very few websites will make the "three-second" cut (the green area). Only Citibank, Google, UPS, FedEx, and Adobe fall under the three-second threshold on a 3G network. Companies that want to ensure that their websites *feel* faster than competitive websites should set strict weight limits. Try to keep your website weight under 1MB.

Facebook's 2G Tuesdays

In October 2015, Facebook began offering employees the ability to experience the internet through a slower 2G network connection, by throttling its internal network. It didn't do this to frustrate employees but to give them a taste of how millions of people currently experience the internet.

Facebook recently launched Facebook Lite, an app that weighs less than 1MB and is intended for these emerging markets.

The app has been hugely successful, even in more developed markets, by people who are concerned about their data consumption.

By understanding the number of smartphone users in a country, along with the speeds of their network connections, you can develop more realistic usage goals for your mobile websites.

Follow the smartphones

For those of us living in developed markets, it may seem like everyone carries a smartphone these days. And yet only half of the 7.2 billion mobile subscribers around the world currently use a smartphone. The rest rely on feature phones that offer little or no internet access.

What does this mean for you? It means learning just how many people have smartphones in each market you target. The good news is that there is an increasing number of countries in which more than half of all people carry a smartphone. But the names of these countries might surprise you.

Shown below, based on Google data, is a list of markets that have 70% or greater penetration of smartphones among all mobile users.

Country	Smartphone Penetration
UAE	91%
Singapore	88%
Saudi Arabia	86%
South Korea	83%
Sweden	83%
Spain	80%
Hong Kong	79%
Norway	79%
Taiwan	78%
Australia	77%
Netherlands	76%

Ireland	75%
Israel	75%
China	74%
Denmark	74%
New Zealand	72%
Switzerland	72%
Malaysia	71%
United Kingdom	71%

If you're looking for the United States, it only has smartphone penetration of 57 percent. The reason I mention this is because many Americans tend to view the world through a desktop-centric point of view. That is, because desktop computers are so widespread, we often imagine users around the world viewing our websites through similar-sized screens.

But most developing markets have limited desktop penetration, which means smartphones are the *only* means of accessing your website. Your mobile website is more important than your desktop website in these *mobile-first* markets. As such, a mobile-first global strategy prioritizes latency and language.

The mobile app myth

Most companies are better served by focusing on improving their mobile websites than launching new mobile apps—because the odds of smartphone users actually using those apps is not good.

According to Nielsen, smartphone users spent more than 37 hours per month on their mobile apps in 2014, a major increase from 23 hours in 2012. But the average number of apps on a user's smartphone has not increased over the same three years, remaining steady at an average of 26 apps.

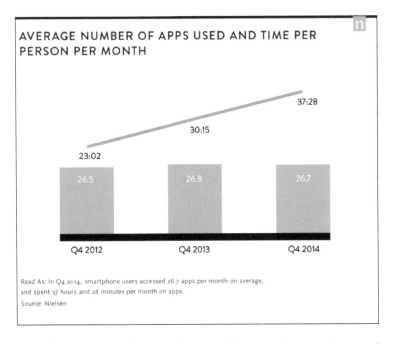

AVERAGE NUMBER OF APPS USED AND TIME PER PERSON PER MONTH

37:28

30:15

23:02

26.5 | 26.8 | 26.7

Q4 2012   Q4 2013   Q4 2014

Read As: In Q4 2014, smartphone users accessed 26.7 apps per month on average, and spent 37 hours and 28 minutes per month on apps.
Source: Nielsen

And these apps are heavily dominated by social networking and entertainment apps. If you do decide to invest in a mobile app, you need to think of your mobile website as the "on ramp" to your app, as this is likely to be how users discover your mobile app in the first place. So invest the time in making sure your mobile website is just as user friendly as your mobile app.

Questions to ask when creating a mobile web strategy

- What is the smartphone penetration within a market?
- What is the network penetration (3G vs. 4G)? The speed of the network plays a fundamental role in the

user experience. As a general rule, if you develop your local website to be lightweight enough to perform well on a 3G wireless network, you will be well positioned to succeed around the world.

- How do people pay for network access? If people are paying for network access by the megabyte, they may be keenly sensitive to any graphics-intensive website. By keeping your website austere and fast-loading, you will ease any worries your customers may have of breaking through their digital ceiling by spending time on your website.

- What is your weight limit? You need to set a limit. And if you want to set separate limits for different markets based on network connections, that's fine too. Just make sure you set limits and that your teams don't exceed them.

- What do users need from your mobile website, and where do they need it? Because mobile users are so *mobile*, you can provide location-specific services that your desktop website cannot.

THINK LOCALLY

Now that you understand how to think
globally, it's time to think locally.

Think "locale"

A locale can mean many things, but for our purposes, it refers to a specific combination of language and region, such as English/ United States or French/Canada. It is important not to confuse language with region, or vice versa. A country, such as Canada, can have more than one locale (French Canada and English Canada), and a language is hardly limited to just one country.

To see a locale in action, visit Microsoft.com, and you'll see this URL: www.microsoft.com/en-us (note the *en-us* locale text at the end of the address). If you were to navigate to the Russian home page, you'd see *en-us* change to *ru-ru* as shown here:

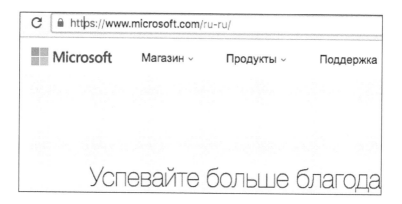

Your phone, your web browser, and even your computer operating system all rely on locale codes to provide you with an experience aligned with your location and language preference. Such as:

Japanese/Japan	www.microsoft.com/ja-jp
Arabic/Egypt	www.microsoft.com/ar-eg
Spanish/Spain	www.microsoft.com/es-es
Spanish/Mexico	www.microsoft.com/es-mx

A locale refers to much more than just a language or region; it refers to the environment your users live within—their norms, laws, customs, and currencies. When developing a website or app for each locale, ask the following questions:

- How are dates displayed?

- How are numbers displayed?

- What is the official currency?

- What's the text direction (left to right, horizontal or vertical)? Arabic languages move from right to left (except for the numbers, which go from left to right).

- What are the sorting and collating rules? For example, there is no such concept as "alphabetization" in Chinese.

- How should search engines work? Once again, Asian languages don't sort like alphabetic languages; they are sorted by number of strokes used.

- What is the default paper size? What if users want to print out your company's web pages? A lot of companies provide PDF files for download. How will these files print on users' computers?

- Do you ask users to input any specific characters that are not available in that given language? Keep in mind that keyboards vary by locale.

- What is the level of bandwidth for your locale? Do users have slow or fast internet connections?

While there are clear boundaries between countries, languages easily cross boundaries. The locale code allows you to freely share one language across borders, such as Spanish across most Latin American markets. While there are clear differences in Spanish across these countries, many companies will develop a more "universal" translation of Spanish that is free of regionalisms, and this can work well across borders.

Of BRICs and Bananas

Locales provide a means for organizing the world, and so do acronyms like MENA (Middle East North Africa) and APAC (Asia Pacific). Companies organize countries together by geographic proximity or economic similarity in order to better manage internal resources. One of the most popular acronyms over the past decade is BRIC (Brazil, Russia, India, China), an acronym coined to describe the four most promising emerging economies. While these four countries have little in common linguistically or even culturally, they do share in their *emerging* status.

And did you know about MINT (Mexico, Indonesia, Nigeria, Turkey)? This is another acronym for the next wave of emerging markets.

And let's not forget MIST (Mexico, Indonesia, South Korea, Turkey). If you think MIST sounds odd, consider CIVETS (Colombia, Indonesia, Vietnam, Egypt, Turkey, South Africa).

But I'm partial to the Blue Banana, shown below (excerpted from the TNT website):

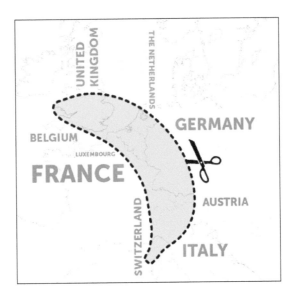

According to Wikipedia, "the Blue Banana is a discontinuous corridor of urbanization in Western Europe, with a population of around 111 million." And if a Blue Banana isn't strange enough, how about a Golden Banana? Yes, it exists as well.

My point here is to emphasize how important labels are in helping us organize the world in ways that better help us address the world. But keep in mind that labels have *limits*.

A locale should not be viewed as the destination, but a step along the way. Once you know a customer's locale you still know very little about that customer, such as gender, age, ethnicity, religion, buying power, favorite color, and favorite sports teams. In other words, don't confuse standards for stereotypes.

With translation, less is less

I began my professional career as a copywriter.

Much of my work focused on direct mail, and I learned early on that *more* text almost always sold better than *less* text. I would conduct tests between four-page sales letters and eight-page sales letters, and the longer sales letters almost always performed better because I had more space to describe the product and its benefits. In direct mail, where there is much risk associated with making a purchase, people want to know everything about a product before they buy it.

Today we have websites, which in many ways function like direct mail packages. Your goal is to quickly catch someone's attention, build trust, and then provide them with enough information for them to make a confident buying decision.

We're told that people don't really read web pages; they skim them. And that's true—to a point. We skim websites in order to quickly find what we're looking for. But when we find what we're looking for, we slow down; we read more carefully. Particularly if this is our first-time purchase with a vendor.

A global consumer electronics company I worked with discovered that if they inserted a link to a downloadable PDF user manual next to the product description, sales increased. It turns out that many people would download the manuals to get an idea of whether they could actually operate the product before they purchased it. User reviews provide another valuable input that customers will read, often quite closely, before clicking *Checkout*. And the best thing about websites is, unlike with direct mail, there are no word-count limits.

But when it comes to localizing that web page, marketing executives are not nearly so generous with word count. And the reason why comes down to dollars and cents.

Translation can be expensive. It can cost $.35 per word to translate from English into Japanese. Now imagine you've got 5,000 words to translate; you're looking at $1,750. Multiply this by twenty languages, and you're now looking at $35,000.

When you include support documentation, user manuals, help content, and legal content, companies easily surpass 100,000 words. And this doesn't include new content or changed content. It's not hard to exceed a million dollars in translation costs to support 20 languages. And yet I can easily make the case that this million dollars is money well spent.

Local websites vs. local façades

While more local content is generally preferable to less local content, what matters most is how you manage user expectations. That is, does your website create the impression that there is more local or translated content than there actually is, thereby disappointing the visitor? You don't want to create what I call a "local façade" (a translated home page with little else translated beneath it).

As you'll see below, Hyatt lets visitors to its Portuguese and Russian websites know that these two sites are "abridged." While marketing teams might resist telling visitors there is *less* content available, such transparency is a smart strategy.

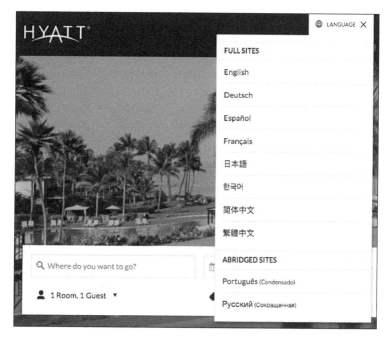

You don't often get a second chance to make a first impression; if people visit your local site and find little there, they won't soon be coming back. So if all you have initially is a mini-site that supports a few basic tasks, such as contacting a local salesperson, requesting a brochure, and so forth, be sure to let your visitors know this. Too often companies view local websites as failures simply because they never created local websites of value.

Do you skimp on English content?

The value of an English-language website is considered self-evident. It's only when the discussion turns to the localization of that website that the value of translation comes under fire.

What I often ask companies before we begin talking about translation costs is to first put a price on the creation of all of the source language content, which is usually English. It's important to understand what you've invested on your primary website, as well as apps and collateral materials, to place the costs of any localization efforts in better context.

I'm not suggesting you shouldn't align your translation costs with expectations. You absolutely should. In fact, I sometimes advise starting slowly and focusing more on mini-sites to help companies manage costs and goals. But if you cut corners on your translation, expect visitors to cut corners on your website.

What's your global gateway strategy?

The global gateway is how people around the world find their local content. There are four tools that companies use to make this process seamless, shown here:

1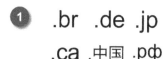
.br .de .jp
.ca .中国 .pф

Country Codes & IDNs
Country code top-level domains (ccTLDs) take users directly to country-specific sites, bypassing .com. Internationalized domain names (IDNs) provide non-Latin domains for countries such as China, Russia and Egypt.

2

Visual Global Gateway
The global gateway includes all visual elements that a user interacts with to select or change a locale (language and/or country). Every web page should support a visual global gateway.

3
68.111.115.24
www.website.de

Geolocation
The web server detects a user's location based on the device IP address and responds with location-specific content. Geolocation should not be used as a standalone solution.

4
lang="de"
website.com/de

Language Negotiation
The web server detects the language preference of the web browser and responds with matching language, if available.

In the Think Globally section I mentioned the importance of country codes in making local websites more discoverable. Country codes provide a local front door to your local websites. But what if your visitors first go to your global .com website? Fortunately, there are three other elements that companies use to improve global navigation:

- The visual global gateway
- Geolocation
- Content negotiation

The visual global gateway

Before you use either geolocation or language negotiation, you must have a user-friendly visual gateway in place. Doing so allows users to self-select their locale.

Many companies get a little too fancy with their global gateways. They often use flags, which I recommend avoiding and will explain later in Think Visually. They also sometimes bury the link to the global gateway menu in the footer of the website, which I also do not recommend.

As shown here, I recommend using a generic globe icon to draw attention to the global gateway menu. Shown here is the header from the GE mobile website:

Second, I recommend a text-based global gateway menu that

displays the locale names in the local languages, when the languages are supported. For example, here is the Microsoft gateway:

When in doubt, geolocate

Let's say you're on your phone and you open up your weather app and it somehow knows where you are.

That's geolocation.

Or you're on a travel website and it knows what your nearest airport is.

Once again, geolocation.

Or you're traveling in Japan and you visit <u>Google.com</u> and you see the search engine greet you with the Japanese website:

Geolocation allows companies to determine the location of the web user so the website may respond with locally relevant content. Companies like Google and Facebook use geolocation to identify the location of the user based on the IP address of the user's computer or mobile device.

More than half of the websites studied in the *Web Globalization Report Card* use geolocation for improving global navigation.

In some cases, a website will automatically redirect users to the country website in which the user resides. This strategy can be dangerous because sometimes your users are traveling outside of their home country.

In other cases, the website will alert users to the availability of a local website without redirecting them.

For example, a German user who visits <u>Amazon.com</u> first sees this screen:

Amazon honors the user intent by displaying the <u>Amazon.com</u> website, but also gives users a one-click option for going to the German website. Amazon does this because it is keenly aware that some users may be Americans abroad and actually want to visit the English-language website.

Geolocation can be particularly handy in mobile scenarios—saving the user from navigating lengthy global gateway menus. But geolocation is not perfect. Users may visit your website via a proxy connection that makes it appear as if they are in a different location, which is common across many corporate networks.

Language negotiation

Language negotiation, also known as language detection, is a technology that delivers users content in the language they want—before they ask for it. And, for the most part, the technology is quite accurate about language preference because it looks at the language setting of the user's mobile device or computer. But be aware that users around the world may speak more than one language and prefer to interact with your website in a different language than you assumed.

Don't view language detection or geolocation as replacements for a visual global gateway but rather as an extension of your global gateway. The visual global gateway ensures that users can easily override whatever locale preference you've detected.

I've just covered the key aspects of a global gateway strategy, and, believe it or not, one can write an entire book about this subject, which I did: *The Art of the Global Gateway*.

There is not one perfect global gateway strategy for all websites. The strategy you use will depend on your customers and how many websites you support. But by knowing what tools you have available, you are off to a great start.

All commerce is local

According to Pitney Bowes, more than one billion people shop online every year, a number that is expected to grow 15% annually.

And in 2016, according to PayPal, 130 million people shopped online across borders, spending more than $300 billion. That's more than double the number from 2013.

As people become more comfortable ordering from abroad, those websites that do the best job of ecommerce localization will be best positioned to succeed in the decades ahead.

Top Currencies					
$	United States Dollars	$	Canadian Dollars	$	Australian Dollars
€	Euro	£	UK Pounds		
All Currencies					
$	Argentinian Pesos	Rp	Indonesian Rupiah	lei	Romanian New Leu
$	Australian Dollars	₪	Israeli New Shekels	p.	Russian Rubles
Tk	Bangladesh Taka	$	Jamaican Dollars	﷼	Saudi Arabian Riyals
R$	Brazilian Reais	¥	Japanese Yen	S$	Singapore Dollars
$	Canadian Dollars	د.ك	Kuwaiti Dinar	R	South African Rand
$	Chilean Pesos	Lt	Lithuanian Litas	₩	South Korean Won

Currency is step one

Displaying products in the local currency is a big first step, but just one step. You also want to support the preferred payment methods of your customers, and you can't assume that Visa or MasterCard alone will suffice. When building ecommerce support, consider the following:

- Currency/payment systems
  - Manage foreign exchange calculations so consumers know when charges will be posted

- Shipping costs
  - Can you offer free shipping?
  - Can customers track their packages in real time?

- Returns
  - Do you pay return shipping? How quickly will returns be processed?

- Customer support
  - ° Do you support language-specific chat, phone, text, email, and/or social platforms?
- Taxes/VAT

Bank transfer
A majority of German and Dutch customers prefer to pay by bank transfer over credit cards. In Germany, GiroPay (www.giropay.de) allows customers to pay by transferring money from their bank accounts. In the Netherlands, the major bank transfer provider is iDEAL (www.ideal.nl). iDEAL reports that more than 20% of transaction volume is used to purchase foreign goods and services.

Cash on delivery (COD)
Customers in many countries prefer to purchase online and pay when the goods are delivered. These countries include China, Vietnam, and Italy.

In Japan, the konbini payment method is very popular; konbini (which means *convenience store*) allows customers to purchase online, then pay for and pick up the products at their local convenience store, such as 7-Eleven. There are more than 19,000 7-Elevens in Japan, more than twice the number that are in the US.

eWallet

In the US, Apple Pay and PayPal offer eWallet apps, and they are slowly gaining momentum. But outside the US the technology has already gone mainstream, particularly in China, where AliPay, backed by Alibaba, enables consumers to use eWallet to accomplish their COD needs.

In Japan, Apple Pay now supports the Suica transit card so people can pay for all transit via contactless payments.

Ecommerce and fulfillment platforms

Given the range of payment options out there, many companies sell through popular marketplaces, including:

- Amazon

- eBay

- MercadoLibre (Latin America)

- Rakuten (Japan)

- Tmall (China; operated by Alibaba)

- Yandex (Russia)

There are also a number of vendors to assist with managing global currency and fulfillment, including:

- Borderfree (owned by Pitney Bowes)

- FedEx

- PayPal

- UPS

- Worldpay

As shown below, Macy's relies on Borderfree to ship to 100 countries.

When is free shipping not free?

Shipping is not free when you're selling goods in France, which recently barred Amazon from offering free shipping. So now Amazon charges EUR 0,01 to ship books, shown on the following page.

The lesson here is that there is no such thing as a global template for ecommerce, as every country offers up unique challenges and regulations.

Partager

Acheter neuf
EUR 20,50
Tous les prix incluent la TVA.

Livraison à EUR 0,01 en France métropolitaine.

En stock.
Expédié et vendu par Amazon.
Emballage cadeau disponible.

Quantité : 1

Ajouter au panier

Identifiez-vous pour activer la commande 1-Click.

Acheter d'occasion
EUR 13,92

Not looking to expand outside of the US yet?
Consider this research from PayPal: *US-based retail websites are the most popular destinations for international consumers.*

China, the UK, and Germany are the top three countries shopping on US websites. You may not be looking for international customers, but they may be looking for you. How will you choose to greet them when they arrive?

Avoiding abandoned shopping carts

Shown below are four similar shipping forms for four countries:

Even though these four checkout forms serve the same purpose, they appear very different. That's because addresses vary significantly across countries. And so do names.

When is a last name not last?

Family name, surname, last name. It all varies by country and culture. Below I've included four names and circled the "last" names in red.

Teresa del Carmen Bustamente de la Fuentes

Jamal aldin Yusuf bin Yaqub al Mekki

Lin Pei Yun

Madras Ramanathan Seshadri

You might consider simply asking users to enter their "full name" instead of first and last, which also creates a shorter checkout form. The shorter the checkout form, the higher the rate of completion—and this holds true for *all* countries.

As you plan your global expansion, your input forms, your databases, your customer support and shipping systems—everything must support the conventions of a given country and culture. It's not easy, and it almost always takes more time and money than companies expect.

Spanish: The second language of the US

According to the US Census, there were 56.6 million Hispanics living in the US as of July 2015, making people of Hispanic origin the nation's largest minority. Hispanics constitute 17.6 percent of the nation's total population. Of this group, an estimated 40 million speak Spanish at home.

One out of four companies in the *Web Globalization Report Card* explicitly support Spanish on their US websites, such as Chevrolet, shown here:

Here are a few of the hundreds of companies that now offer Spanish-language websites for the US market:

- Allstate
- American Airlines
- Bank of America
- ESPN
- Ford
- Geico
- H&R Block
- Southwest Airlines
- Verizon Wireless
- Walgreens
- Disney

According to *Ad Age*, US Hispanics have a buying power of $1.7 trillion. As the buying power of this market grows, companies have responded with translated signage, packaging, advertising, and websites.

When developing Spanish-language apps and sites for the US market, keep the following tips in mind:

- Support social platforms in the local language. More than 31 million US Hispanics use Facebook and Messenger each month.

- Avoid location-specific or culture-specific visual clichés, such as pictures of sombreros and margaritas.

- Make local contact information (phone, email) easy to find. Explicitly note if you offer Spanish-language phone and email support.

- When translating into Spanish, understand that there are different *flavors* of Spanish, such as Cuban, Mexican, and Puerto Rican. You may want to target a specific group of Spanish speakers or you may work toward a more *universal* Spanish that works across these different groups; most US companies focus on supporting universal Spanish.

- When linking to your localized site, use *Español* not *Spanish*.

You say Czech Republic; I say Czechia

Thinking locally is a never-ending process. Because the world is changing constantly, including even country names.

For years now, the Czech Republic has had no official "short name." But the Czech Republic is now in the process of promoting Czechia as its shorter name.

As of this writing, the changeover isn't official. There are some within the government who feel that Czechia is too similar to Chechnya (the Russian republic). But the fact that the country name *could* change is just one example of how challenging it can be to think locally on a global scale.

And what does a country's name change mean to a US company?

It could mean quite a lot.

You'll have to update your global gateway and the country menu on your ecommerce forms, and you'll need to update every country name reference on your localized website.

There are two takeaways here: First, even something seemingly as permanent as a country name can change. Myanmar was known once as Burma; Mumbai was once Bombay.

The second takeaway is this: *Thinking locally requires seeing the world through your customer's eyes.*

Exonyms vs. Endonyms

An exonym (*exo* meaning outside) is the external name for a place, people, or a language. For example, *Spanish* is an exonym. An endonym (*endo* meaning inside) is the opposite: how members of a group refer to themselves, their language, and so on. *Español* is an endonym.

I often come across websites with global gateway menus that list country names as follows:

- Finland
- Germany
- Spain

But these are exonyms, when what should be displayed are endonyms:

- Suomi

- Deutschland

- España

This may seem like a minor detail, but it often sheds light on a larger issue—the inability to see the country or region through the eyes of its residents. When visitors to a website see a country list full of exonyms, they may rightfully suspect that they are not high-priority customers. Not yet, at least.

```
Argentina
Armenia
Austria
Belgium
Bosnia
Brazil
China
Bulgaria
Chile
Colombia
Croatia
Denmark
Dominican Republic
Ecuador
El Salvador
Faroe Islands
Fiji
Finland
France
Germany
Guadeloupe
Guatemala
Guam
```

THINK CULTURALLY

Cultures are not limited by geographic borders, nor are they limited by language.

Cultures visible and invisible

A culture includes the collective beliefs, customs, arts, and sports of particular society or group. And a group may include a nation, region, province, city, or something even more specific—say, the culture of Boston Red Sox baseball fans.

And culture isn't always easy to see.

Just as you can't assume that every American loves apple pie, you can't assume every citizen of France drinks wine.

But awareness of culture can make all the difference between success and failure. As you'll see on the following pages, every culture is a whole new world to be explored and understood.

Holidays

In the introduction, I mentioned the significance of Singles Day to Chinese consumers. But by far the most important holiday in China is the New Year's celebration, and it is only in the past few years that non-Chinese multinationals have fully embraced this holiday. Here is a view of Apple's New Year's promotion from 2015:

Starbucks now regularly releases a special promotion for the New Year. The color red, widely viewed as a celebratory and auspicious color across Asia, features prominently.

Diwali

In India, the festival of lights, known as Diwali, occupies the month of October and is responsible for a surge in online sales, particularly as Indians try to avoid crowds.

Flipkart has long been the dominant ecommerce retailer in India, but Amazon is no longer content to remain in second place. In 2016, Amazon launched its Great Indian Festival promotion with free prizes including a number of cars, even a free house.

Amazon claimed record sales and one billion hits, which is about as precise as Amazon gets in releasing internal data. But the fact that Amazon is so heavily invested in India is evidence enough of the long-term potential for international retailers.

And this holiday isn't just about retailers but any global company. Like Chevrolet, which in 2016 offered a free gold coin for purchases made during festival season:

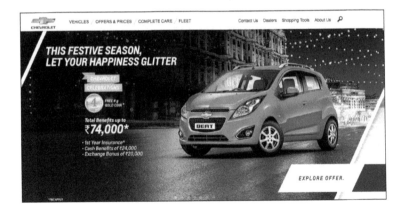

Halloween

Halloween is one of those holidays that means different things to different people. As well as to different countries. And the list of countries that celebrate Halloween continues to grow.

What started as a largely European tradition morphed into an American retail obsession. And because of the retail revenues, it's no surprise that this holiday has gone global. Here's a screen grab from Woolworths Australia:

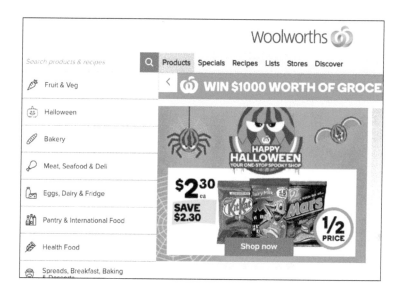

Latin Americans also celebrate Halloween; here is a screen grab from Metro in Peru:

And Falabella in Colombia:

And, of course, Japan has long been an eager celebrant of this holiday. This from Rakuten:

From Australia to Germany to Chile and Peru, Halloween is big business.

Black Friday & Cyber Monday

The days after Thanksgiving used to be primarily US-centric retailer promotions, but retailers have been taking them global. Even though Canada celebrates its Thanksgiving a month earlier than Americans, most Canadian retailers celebrate Black Friday.

Amazon has made a concerted effort to promote Black Friday in the UK since 2012 and has since added a number of additional countries, including France and Mexico, shown on the following page.

In 2016, Alibaba began promoting Black Friday to its Chinese customers. Cyber Monday is celebrated in Canada, the UK, Brazil, Germany, and other markets.

Click Frenzy
Launched in 2012, this holiday, inspired by Cyber Monday, is an Australian shopping day, held on the third Tuesday in November. Learn more at www.clickfrenzy.com.au.

Golden Week
Both Japan and China celebrate a Golden Week holiday, though at different times of the year: April/May for Japan and October for China. This is the most popular time for travel, and more than half a billion Chinese travel during this holiday.

Valentine's Day

Valentine's Day has become another global holiday—celebrated in Russia, Germany, and Japan, among others—yet it's not celebrated on the same day (or in the same way) in all parts of the world. In Brazil, the day is known as *Dia dos Namorados* (Lover's Day) and is celebrated on June 12 (so as not to conflict with Carnival). Taiwan has two Valentine's Day celebrations: February 14 and July 7.

White Day

In Japan and South Korea, women give gifts on February 14, with men returning the favor a month later on a day known as White Day.

Keeping up on local holidays

It's not easy to know which holidays are happening where at all times. But there are a number of resources to help, such as:

- www.officeholidays.com
- www.timeanddate.com/holidays

Lucky numbers

Most people have a lucky number. So do cultures. In the US, the number 13 is considered so unlucky that you'd have a hard time finding an elevator with a 13th floor button. And the number 13 is about 15% less likely to appear in a house price than either 12 or 14.

Numbers play a particularly important role in the pricing of products. Shown below is an excerpt from Apple US:

Space Gray	Space Gray	Space Gray
New	New	New
2.0GHz Processor	Touch Bar and Touch ID	Touch Bar and Touch ID
256GB Storage	2.9GHz Processor	2.9GHz Processor
	256GB Storage	512GB Storage
2.0GHz dual-core Intel Core i5 processor	2.9GHz dual-core Intel Core i5 processor	2.9GHz dual-core Intel Core i5 processor
Turbo Boost up to 3.1GHz	Turbo Boost up to 3.3GHz	Turbo Boost up to 3.3GHz
8GB 1866MHz memory	8GB 2133MHz memory	8GB 2133MHz memory
256GB PCIe-based SSD	256GB PCIe-based SSD	512GB PCIe-based SSD
Intel Iris Graphics 540	Intel Iris Graphics 550	Intel Iris Graphics 550
Two Thunderbolt 3 ports	Four Thunderbolt 3 ports	Four Thunderbolt 3 ports
	Touch Bar and Touch ID	Touch Bar and Touch ID
$1,499.00	$1,799.00	$1,999.00
Up to 18 months of special financing	Up to 18 months of special financing	Up to 18 months of special financing

In Western countries, it's quite common to price items at, say, $1,499 rather than $1,500. While I'm not sure doing so convinces anyone that the product is significantly less expensive, the practice is almost considered standard.

Now let's look at how those same three computers are priced in China:

Instead of repeated 9s we see repeated 8s. There is nothing inherently wrong with using the number 9 in China; in fact, the numbers 9 and 6 are also considered lucky numbers in China. But the number 8 stands far above the rest in the good fortune department.

That's because the Chinese pronunciation of eight is similar to the word that means *prosperity* or *wealth*. In China, license plates with multiple 8s are highly valued and can fetch million-dollar prices.

And when it comes to pricing high-ticket items, it's never a bad idea to make that high number as *lucky* as possible. This phenomenon is not unique to high-end electronics. According to the real estate company Trulia, home listings in Asian-majority neighborhoods are significantly more likely to end in the number eight.

Unlucky number 4

If there is one number to avoid throughout Asia, it's the number four. When pronounced, it sounds similar to the word for *death*. Many buildings in Asia don't have a fourth floor, and some don't have a 14th floor (the four and the ten are considered a particularly ominous combination).

I've assembled a list of lucky and unlucky numbers across a handful of countries around the world. Keep in mind that there are always exceptions to the rule.

	Lucky	Unlucky
China	6, 8, 9	4, 7
US	7	13
Russia	3, 7	13, 6
Korea	7	4
Italy	3, 7	13, 17
Norway	9	13
Sweden	3	13
Ireland	4	13
France		9
Germany		13, 4
Philippines		13

Certain number combinations also figure prominently in various cultures. For example, in the US Bible Belt region, homes are 27% more likely to include 316 in the price, a reference to the New Testament verse John 3:16. In Nevada, a region quite familiar with its gaming industry, it's not uncommon to see owners list their homes with triple sevens—a winning line in a slot machine.

Numbers and branding

While prices can often be quickly tweaked as needed, brand names (and any numbers they include) cannot. If, for example, you're launching a fourth-generation product, you might avoid using the number 4 in the brand name if you're considering the Asian market. Years ago, the computer device maker Palm avoided calling the successor to the Palm 3 the Palm 4 because of concerns over Asia.

Lucky and unlucky letters

According to a study published in the *Journal of Consumer Marketing*, not only is 8 considered lucky across China, so too are the letters A and S. Conversely, the number 4 is joined by the letters F and Z in the unlucky category. While the numbers have significance based on how they sound when pronounced, the letters are significant based on their position in the alphabet as well as their association with educational grade. But the key findings of the study are that products with lucky alpha-numeric brand names were thought to be "luckier, and have better quality and greater success than those with unlucky brand names."

Of course, the luckiest prices are often the lowest prices. Consumers will see a different form of luck in a price that's well below the competition.

Why translate when you can transcreate?

With translation, the goal is to accurately convey the meaning of the source text into the target text. If you're translating instructions for how to use a medical device, a literal translation is desirable. That is, you don't want the translator to "get creative."

However, if you're translating a website, you don't always want a literal, word-for-word translation. You want your messages to feel natural to the end users, and this might require *transcreation*.

Transcreation (creative translation) walks a delicate line between translation and content creation. Transcreation is typically charged at a higher per-word rate and generally requires translators with a strong marketing or copywriting skillset.

Companies are becoming more sophisticated in how they purchase translation services. They may hire one translation vendor for the word-for-word translation of their legal documents and product spec sheets, then hire a separate translation firm for the transcreation of the marketing messages.

Also, as companies rely on in-house writers around the world to manage their blogs and social feeds, these writers are playing a major role in transcreating messages that come from headquarters. Content that is created closest to the consumer tends to be the most effective content. That's because the content creators (who are typically native speakers and residents of the market) understand the nuances of the market, the latest slang, and demographic subtleties.

The key message to keep in mind as you manage your company's content localization is that not all content should be translated the same way. Some content may need translation, while other content may require a complete rethinking at the local level—that is, transcreation.

What's most significant about the rise in transcreation services is that marketing executives are now taking a closer look at the content itself, its audiences, and its intended ROI. And this is a good thing, because every language should be treated as a new language, not just a translated copy of English.

Creating "world-ready" text

As your source language becomes translated or transcreated, you need to ensure that this text is "world ready" before it goes to translators. World-ready text is free of anything that is too closely tied to one culture or country. For example, if you say customers will "hit a home run" with a product, understand that this phrase won't mean much to people unfamiliar with baseball.

When creating global English, keep it "plain"

In 2010 the US government passed a law mandating the use of plain language in government communications. In other words, the government was ordering itself to keep things simple.

When it comes to creating global content, *plain* language is much easier to translate. As a general rule, if your translator is having trouble understanding your content, you'd better rewrite it first.

An entire field of research and software has risen up around the need to create content that is easier to understand and easier to translate. There's even a Center for Plain Language (www. centerforplainlanguage.org)

Here are some tips to keep in mind when creating world-ready content:

- Keep sentences short. Longer sentences are more difficult to translate and understand. They often contain multiple ideas that are better left in individual sentences.

- Keep paragraphs short. Brief, logically ordered sections of content help users quickly digest and understand what you're trying to communicate.

- Use strong verbs. Avoid the passive voice.

- Maintain a conversational tone. Write as you would address your customer in person.

- Avoid jargon. You may know the technical term for a specific product or service, but odds are your customers don't.

- Avoid culture references. Baseball and movie references don't travel well outside the United States. Stay focused on the product or service.

There are now software applications, such as Acrolinx (www.acrolinx.com), that help content creators follow these guidelines, providing real-time suggestions and even helping them reuse content. While an author of a novel wants to avoid repeating the same phrase, the author of a "how to" document should reuse a phrase instead of trying to say the same thing ten different ways. Doing so adds to translation costs and risks confusing readers.

Reuse translation through "memory"

Translation memory (TM) software is widely used by companies to save previous translations and leverage them as more content is translated. This way, previously translated phrases and sentences can be re-used, improving consistency and lowering translation costs. Terminology management software also helps with maintaining consistent use of terms across all languages.

Just don't do it

Slogans and taglines are particularly difficult to translate literally. For example, years ago Dell wanted to translate its slogan "Easy as Dell" for Japan. A literal translation didn't make much sense to users, so the slogan was transcreated to mean "Simple for you, Dell," which appealed to the local market. This may sound like a minor adjustment, but a great deal of effort went into it. Nike tried to translate its "Just Do It" slogan but ultimately gave up and kept the slogan in English worldwide. I now recommend that companies avoid global slogans altogether.

The obligatory lost in translation chapter

When you've been in this business as long as I have, your eyes blur over when you come across another viral article poking fun at some mistranslation a company made in some part of the world.

And yet when I share some of these stories with people outside of this industry I am reminded that most people don't appreciate how wrong translation can go.

So here are a few mistranslation classics from over the years:

- In Taiwan, the translation of the Pepsi slogan "Come alive with the Pepsi Generation" came out as "Pepsi will bring your ancestors back from the dead."

- Also in Chinese, the Kentucky Fried Chicken slogan "finger-lickin' good" came out as "eat your fingers off."

- Ford had a similar problem in Brazil when the Pinto flopped. The company found out that Pinto was Brazilian slang for "tiny male genitals."

- When Parker Pen marketed a ballpoint pen in Mexico, its ads were supposed to say, "It won't leak in your pocket and embarrass you." However, the company mistakenly used the Spanish word "embarazar" for embarrass. Instead the ads said, "It won't leak in your pocket and make you pregnant."

- Chicken-man Frank Perdue's slogan, "It takes a tough man to make a tender chicken," got terribly mangled in another Spanish translation. A photo of Perdue with one of his birds appeared on billboards all over Mexico with a caption that explained, "It takes a hard man to make a chicken aroused."

- In Italy, a campaign for Schweppes Tonic Water translated the name into Schweppes Toilet Water.

- Coors put its slogan, "Turn it loose," into Spanish, where it was read as, "Suffer from diarrhea."

- The name Coca-Cola in China was first rendered as Ke-kou-ke-la. Unfortunately, the Coke company did not discover until after thousands of signs had been printed that the phrase means "bite the wax tadpole" or "female horse stuffed with wax," depending on the dialect. Coke then researched 40,000 Chinese characters and found a close phonetic equivalent, "ko-kou-ko-le," which can be loosely translated as "happiness in the mouth."

- Clairol introduced the "Mist Stick," a curling iron, into German only to find out that "mist" is slang for manure. Not too many people had use for the "manure stick."

- When Gerber started selling baby food in Africa, they used the same packaging as in the US, with the beautiful baby on the label. Later they learned that in Africa, companies routinely put pictures on the label of what's inside, since most people can't read English.

Some brands are foreign by design

How does one localize a French wine or a German car or a Swiss watch?

Answer: *By localizing as little as possible.*

Some companies make the mistake of overlocalizing their products or services for new markets, unaware that their places of origin are elemental to their brands.

The CEO of Starbucks summed it up nicely several years ago when he said, "On a country-by-country basis, the largest hurdle we had to overcome was thinking we had to be different. There are regional differences in every market, but the main reason we are successful in the US is the same as why we are successful internationally."

But Starbucks does indeed localize when it has to. For example, the peak time in China is in the afternoons, not the morning hours. And food preferences vary widely by market. Starbucks does what most companies do when they go global—which is as little as they have to. Localization isn't easy, and less is usually more. Of course, the magic comes from deciding what needs to be localized—and how best to do it.

In China, *foreign* can be a positive

Many European and American companies have learned (sometimes the hard way) that Chinese consumers want to order specific products from foreign companies. Many Chinese consumers are wary of purchasing domestically because they fear purchasing counterfeit goods. Many affluent parents purchase infant diapers from foreign companies because they don't trust domestic producers. This doesn't mean you don't translate your website, but that you may not need to appear too local. This can be a difficult balancing act, but the better you understand your customers the easier it will get.

Faux-local brands

Chinese fortune cookies are a uniquely American invention. Häagen-Dazs is not a foreign brand, but a brand developed in the Bronx to appear foreign.

And even when brands get purchased by foreign companies, they will wisely cling to what made them valuable brands to begin with. Consider Maker's Mark, now owned by a Japanese company, which you won't see mentioned prominently on its website; you will see plenty of photos of its Kentucky distillery.

The key question to ask when entering a new market is: Am I serving a uniquely local need, or am I selling a uniquely foreign product?

THINK VISUALLY

A picture tells a thousand words, and not only in English.

Global design is less design

Suppose you work for Coca-Cola and you've been put in charge of a global website redesign. The first thing you do is take a tour of the company's more than 30 country websites.

Like the France home page, shown here:

Then you visit Argentina, with an entirely different design:

And here is Japan—the bulk of the home page is one looping video:

These three countries have taken strikingly different approaches to their websites. And now you have to face the uncomfortable task of convincing all regional and country offices to support *one* design.

Good luck with that.

I've participated in numerous global website redesigns, and I've witnessed many success stories, but I've also watched companies fail to align their many countries and regions onto a common global design, resulting in ongoing tensions between corporate and country offices.

But the fact is, global consistency is essential to successful globalization. Companies that get this include Apple. Shown below is the home page for France:

And here is Japan:

While it might not seem so at first, global design is also less work. Once you have a global design template in place, the regional and local offices have more time to devote to local content as opposed to managing a unique web design.

In praise of the global template

Your company may be only focused on expanding into one country today, but three years from now you may have 25 country websites to manage. In order to efficiently manage all of these sites, you need a global template. Companies should use global design templates to ensure a consistent user experience and to minimize internal website management costs. A global template need not override local customization; a well-designed website can both be globally consistent and locally flexible.

Many companies have been successfully using global templates for more than a decade, including 3M, IBM, and Google. The global design template is now a widely accepted best practice in web globalization.

I have yet to encounter a company that abandoned its global design template in favor of letting each country or region design its own website from the ground up. Global templates can be particularly valuable to companies that support multiple brands.

Shown below are the home pages of three Marriott hotel brands. Even though the logos, color schemes, and content are different, the underlying templates are similar. You can see the similarities in the header and the placement of the reservation engine. This illustrates how flexible a template can be not just in support of global consistency but brand consistency.

How to get local buy-in for your global template

It is only natural for local offices that have spent years managing their own web designs to resist efforts from above that take away some measure of control. If all of your local offices resist embracing a global design, focus on getting at least one local office to run a pilot project. After the project succeeds, and the local office is freed up to focus on the content itself, enlist this office to help sell the other local offices on the idea. Often, local offices are more open to taking advice from their counterparts.

Finally, be open to the notion that you might have one or two markets that resist embracing the global template. I do find that some global companies give free rein to certain Asian countries because of the unique challenges of these markets. That's fine, just as long as most of your local offices support the template.

When colors clash

We have an intimate relationship with colors. We often dress up in favorite colors. When we leave the house there are colors we recognize without even thinking about them—the color of a stop sign or road sign, the color of money.

Colors carry significant cultural, political, and personal meaning. This chapter takes a high-level look at major colors and their meaning to countries and cultures around the world.

Black

- Black signifies death (and bad luck) in the US and most European countries. In certain contexts, black can also convey sophistication.

- In Africa, black conveys age and wisdom.

White

- In the US, white is synonymous with purity and justice.

- White signifies death across much of Asia.

- In Japan, wrapping a gift in white symbolizes death.

- In Africa, white signifies purity and victory.

Blue

- Blue is probably the *safest* global color, in that most cultures perceive it positively.

- In Israel, blue signifies holiness.

- In Greece, blue is a color of national pride.

- In Ukraine, blue signifies great health.

- In the US, blue signifies justice and trust, but can also signal "feeling blue."

Red

- In the US, red conveys passion and excitement. But red can also be perceived negatively, as in *danger* or *bleeding*. On stock market indices, red means *loss*.

- In South Korea, writing a person's name in red indicates that the person is dead.

- Ironically, across most of Asia red is considered a celebratory and lucky color, used on wedding dresses and money envelopes intended to convey good fortune. The Chinese stock market uses the color red to indicate stocks that have gone up in value, not down. It's no accident that the Apple Watch web page promotes the red band first and foremost.

Green

- Green is globally associated with environmental causes.

- Green is also widely associated with the military.

- In the US, you can be "green with envy"; green is also the color of money.

- Green is considered holy and sacred in Muslim countries; consider the flag for the Kingdom of Saudi Arabia:

- In China, green is used on its stock exchange to indicate stocks that have lost value, the opposite of Western stock exchanges.

Yellow

- In the US, yellow means faith, caution, and hope.

- In Germany, you can be "yellow with envy."

- In Mexico, yellow is the color of mourning.

Pink

- Pink may considered the most feminine color in the US, but outside the US yellow is generally perceived to be more feminine.

Purple

- Purple is widely associated with royalty and spirituality around the globe.

- In Brazil, sending purple flowers is considered an insult.

- Purple signifies death across much of Latin America.

Orange

- In Western countries, orange conveys warmth and signifies autumn.

- In the Netherlands, orange is synonymous with the royal family, as well as the national football team.

- In Southeast Asia, monks wear orange (saffron) robes; Buddhists see orange as illumination, and Hindus view the color as sacred, a sign of fire.

Revolutionary colors

Revolutionary movements have long been associated with colors, such as:

- Pink: Used by Iranian advocates of women's rights and reform.

- Yellow: Used by pro-democracy opponents of Kyrgyzstan's

president, Askar Akayev.

- Blue: Used by potential opponents of President Aleksandr Lukashenko of Belarus.

- Orange: The color that signified the Ukrainian revolution.

- Purple: The color associated with the first Iraqi vote post-Saddam Hussein.

Celebratory colors

Across most of Asia, red is the undisputed color for celebrations. In parts of Latin America it is a New Year's Eve tradition to ring in the new year wearing new underwear. But not just any underwear; the color of the underwear signifies your resolution. For example, yellow means *money* and red means *love*. These colors may not be applied just to underwear but also outerwear and to the color of objects displayed in a home.

Color rule breakers

Despite these color rules there are many case studies of companies that have successfully broken the rules. For example, Apple went into Asia using the same white-heavy packaging it uses in Western markets. Though local convention might have suggested de-emphasizing the color white, Apple stuck with its global aesthetic and today is quite successful across Asia. The company does, however, also emphasize the color red.

Local models

The most culturally loaded images are those of our fellow humans. Our eyes are naturally drawn to photographs of other people, so it's understandable why marketing and web teams are eager to include photographs of people to make websites more engaging and human.

Cosmetics companies, such as Avon and NIVEA, are particularly sensitive to localizing their models to the target audience, such as Japan.

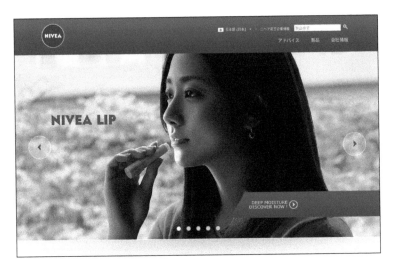

When you include a photograph of a man or woman on your website, you should be acutely aware of all the ways that this person may unintentionally offend your audience around the world. From clothing (or lack of clothing) to ethnicity to posture to gesture, every detail matters.

Just because an image works well on your US website doesn't mean it will work equally well on other country websites. Worse, you could be sending the wrong message to your customers without intending to do so. When expanding to new markets, these photographs must be carefully vetted beforehand by local teams.

When targeting the Middle East, companies need to be particularly sensitive to cultural standards for clothing. Consider the NIVEA Middle East home page:

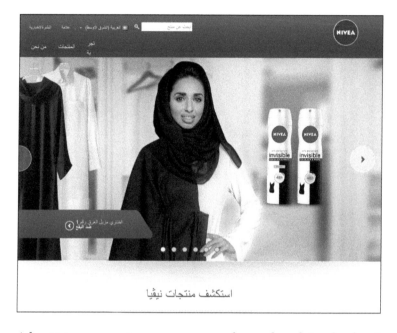

Advertising campaigns are commonly produced in the local markets using local models. Yet websites have historically been exempted from this practice in favor of relying on global stock images. But this is fortunately changing, and quickly.

The language of the body

Body language is loaded with cultural meaning—and often can send conflicting cultural messages. Consider the following gestures and how they are perceived in various cultures.

Winston Churchill popularized this gesture as the *V for victory* sign during the Second World War. In the US, during the 1960s, the gesture came to mean *peace*. However, this gesture, when the palm faces inward, becomes obscene in the U.K. and other British territories.

Thumbs up has evolved into a very positive gesture throughout North America. However, in most of the Middle East and parts of Africa, this gesture can be vulgar. In Japan, the thumb is considered the fifth digit; a raised thumb will order five of something.

While this gesture means *a-okay* or *all is well* in the US, in France it signifies *zero* or *nothing*. In Denmark or Italy it can be taken as an insult. In Brazil, Guatemala, and Paraguay, it may be considered obscene.

If you put your feet on a table in the Middle East, exposing the soles of your shoes, you are insulting your hosts. Throwing a shoe at someone is an even graver insult. When Saddam Hussein's statue was overthrown in 2013, Iraqis pummeled the statue with their shoes.

You can't know what every gesture means in every country, but by testing your visuals beforehand with cultural experts within the target countries and regions, you'll be sure to minimize any unintentional faux pas.

Taking icons global

In the early 1980s, to make computing less complex and intimidating, Apple launched a graphical user interface (GUI, pronounced *gooey*). This interface made extensive use of icons and helped to revolutionize computing. Gone were the days of cryptic keyboard commands. Using a Macintosh, if a user wanted to delete a file, he or she simply dragged the file to the trash can, which looked a lot like this one:

More than 30 years later, that trash can is still with us, along with a great many more icons. And some of the icons that found adoption on computers have migrated to websites and smartphones. Today, icons are an essential tool for ecommerce, web applications, navigation, and overall usability. But not all icons are equally user friendly, nor do all icons travel equally well globally.

While there is no rule that says icons must remain consistent among websites, there is a larger force at work that compels companies to head in this direction: *the need for usable websites.* The less thinking one must devote to understanding how to use and navigate a website, the greater the odds that the website will be successful. Easily recognizable icons can go a long way toward improving usability.

But icons don't typically become icons overnight. Some icons are easily identified because they are based on physical equivalents, such as the ubiquitous shopping cart icon.

Imitation isn't just flattery, it's a necessity

While designers are apt to try to find new design solutions to old problems, sometimes they are wise to abide by established usability conventions. For example, if you were to design a ticket reservation web application for an airline, you would want to build upon conventions that are used by most other ticket sites.

That's not to say that you cannot innovate, just that it's wise to build upon standards that are already in wide use. As you develop icons for a global audience, keep the following tips in mind:

- Avoid hand gestures. As noted in the previous chapter, hand gestures can be risky. Better to avoid them.

- Which way is forward? Arrows are often used to point the way forward, such as on multi-part forms. But arrows can be tricky because web layouts for Arabic and Hebrew speakers typically flow from right to left.

In this case, moving forward may require an arrow that points in the opposite direction as on a Western-language website.

- What color is your mailbox? To signify *mail*, use an envelope icon instead of a mailbox icon. Mailboxes are red in the UK, Australia, and Japan, and yellow in many other countries, and shapes vary widely.

- Maximum security. Icons can play a valuable role in making a web user feel secure when shopping online. The padlock icon is frequently used to indicate secure and/or encrypted shopping. The use of credit card logos also can improve user confidence.

Testing without text

Another technique to ensure that your website is world-ready is to test your web design or application without using meaningful text. For example, you insert a language you do not understand and see if you can still navigate the website successfully.

Many software companies call this process *pseudo-localization,* and they will insert a special text that includes a range of characters from the world's many languages. Not only does this dummy text help testers look beyond language, it also helps to isolate areas in which text is clipped, which is common when text is translated from one language to another.

The appification of icons

The dominance of smartphones and apps has given rise to a new wave of icons—icons that have migrated over to websites. And as the lines blur between what is an app and what is a website, this migration makes perfect sense. It also benefits users who navigate between websites and mobile apps.

The icon on the left means "settings" and the icon on the right means "menu."

The standardization of the globe icon

Earlier in the book I mentioned that GE uses a generic globe icon to highlight its global gateway. GE is not alone. A growing number of companies are wisely using globe icons for this purpose, such as Enterprise, TNT, and Intel:

What about using a map icon instead? While many websites do use a map icon, I find that maps don't display as well in small sizes. More important, maps are not geopolitically neutral. Some regions may be displayed in the icon while others are not displayed. A generic globe icon has no geopolitical issues.

Conduct a visual audit

To ensure that you go global with minimal problems, I recommend conducting a visual audit of your source language website before handing it off to localizers. An audit takes into account not only the content of the visuals but the manner in which they are deployed. Among the questions a visual audit should answer include:

- Is each image absolutely essential?
  - ° Every image carries a performance penalty, which is particularly important on mobile websites.
  - ° For your global templates, try to avoid using any other image than your logo.
- Is there any embedded text within any of your visuals?
  - ° If so, remove text to accelerate translation workflow and improve SEO performance.
- For icons, do they follow globally established (or informal) standards?
  - ° If not, are the icons clear to users across all of your target markets?
- For photographs of people, does each photograph send the right message? Have you considered their style of dress and body language?
  - ° Have you considered using local models for your local websites?
- Are your colors locally relevant and meaningful?
  - ° Test your colors across all markets, particularly when it comes to product packaging.
- Will your image strategy scale?

○ If you find you're expending great resources to localize images when supporting just a few markets, imagine the challenge of supporting 30 or more markets.

The evolution of a global icon

In December 2005, the International Red Cross & Red Crescent Societies adopted an additional global emblem—the red crystal.

Prior to 2005, as shown below, two different emblems were used to signify humanitarian aid agencies: the red cross (used in the Western world) and the red crescent (used in the Arab world).

While the Red Cross hasn't abandoned its namesake emblems (the red cross and red crescent) it was forced to find a more globally neutral identity in order to be viewed as truly globally friendly.

The evolution of the new red cross icon is a case study in unintended consequences. The red cross was adopted in 1863 by Swiss humanitarians who had simply reversed the colors of the Swiss flag. The goal of the emblem was to be highly identifiable to protect medical personnel from attack during conflicts. Although the intent was not religious, it was taken as such by many cultures.

The Ottoman Empire refused to the use the emblem, adopting instead the red crescent, which was formally admitted alongside the red cross in the 1929 Geneva Conventions. The two emblems are used in more than 190 countries. Israel developed its own type of Red Cross organization, the Magen David Adom (MDA) Society, but it was denied entrance into the International Red Cross because it used the Red Shield of David as its emblem.

This stalemate did not end until the International Committee of the Red Cross (ICRC) and the International Federation of Red Cross and Red Crescent Societies approved the new emblem.

The red crystal now gives aid organizations around the world the option of using a more universal emblem, and it may also be used with the organization's existing emblem.

Shown below is how the MDA Society incorporates the crystal icon for use outside of Israel.

What lessons does the evolution of this icon hold for multinational corporations? It is perfectly understandable that the founders of the Red Cross did not think that their organization would have the global reach that it does today and so did not think through the global implications of their chosen emblem. Today, however, when all websites have global reach from day one, companies need to think globally early on to prevent such awkward and expensive changes down the road.

Wave flags with caution (if at all)

About a year after college I quit my job to backpack with a buddy through Australia. At the time I had read that if you wore an American flag patch on your backpack, you stood a better chance of hitching rides. But it didn't take long after landing in Australia to realize that many Australians were not very fond of us Americans. We quickly removed our patches and, at times, pretended we were Canadian. This was my first lesson on the cultural significance of flags. It would prove not to be the last.

Because flags carry so much historical and cultural meaning, I advise avoiding them—particularly on your website.

Many companies use flags as a navigation aid, and this can create problems, often unintentionally. Flags are sometimes used to indicate language, but many countries have more than one official language and many more unofficial languages.

Taiwan: Country or region?
According the United Nations, Taiwan is an independent country. According to China, Taiwan is a region of China. And if you display

the Taiwan flag on your website, you are effectively weighing in on this argument. Which is fine, if that's your goal. But millions of Chinese do not like to see the Taiwan flag displayed and can be quite vocal about it. Which is one reason some websites display global gateways like this:

Country/Regional Directory

Africa	Available Languages			Availa
Egypt	› English	South Africa		› Engl
Kenya	› English			
Asia				
China	› 中文	Malaysia		› Engl
Taiwan	› 臺灣	Pakistan		› Engl
India	› English	Philippines		› Engl

Notice the missing flag for Taiwan. This is hardly an elegant solution. And it's not just Taiwan that presents this challenge. The flag for Kosovo is also disputed by its neighbors.

Flags limit global reach

Shown below is the gateway for Schiphol airport.

An American who speaks English could visit the site, see the UK flag, and wonder if the content is relevant. In this case, the flag limits the reach of English content.

Flags don't scale

You might include a few flags on your global gateway when you begin expanding your website, but you'll soon realize that flags don't scale well. Apple uses flags, and when viewed on a page, the collage of colors actually works against usability.

If you look closely at the Apple global gateway you'll notice two regions that don't have flags (excerpted below). This is yet another reason why flags are problematic.

One flag you should never use

Just because the UK voted to separate from the EU doesn't mean that it's considering a merger with the United States as this visual might suggest:

I understand why companies use this hybrid flag as an all-purpose *English* icon. But it fails to achieve that goal because flags are not synonymous with language. And, as icons go, people generally don't like to see their national flags chopped up or merged with other flags. A better approach is to avoid using any flag at all and simply use the text "English."

Visually managing language expectations

Following language breadcrumbs

To usability professionals, a *breadcrumb* is a visual navigational aid that helps website visitors find their way.

Shown below is a breadcrumb on the Lenovo website, allowing users to easily navigate from *Home* to *Laptops* to *ThinkPad* and so on.

For international website visitors, language also functions as a breadcrumb, helping visitors navigate their way to their localized websites.

Assume for a moment that you are trying to book a hotel room at this Japanese hotel website (and you don't speak any Japanese).

What do you do when you land on this page?

Odds are that you'll first click on your browser's *back* button, effectively giving up on this website. But let's say you've found the right hotel, just not the right *language*.

So you look for your language. Any little scrap of language will do. Speaking for myself, I'm looking for text such as *English* or United States.

And here it is in the header:

This little breadcrumb is all I need to navigate to my localized website.

It's important to take the time to view your website and software through the eyes of someone who may not speak your default language. Only then will you truly understand the value of language in ensuring that users find what they're looking for.

A user-friendly global gateway is essential to ensuring that a first-time visitor to your website does not hit the *back* button.

Managing expectations on a global gateway

First of all, the country name should be displayed in the local language (when the language is supported). For example, instead of *Germany*, the text should read *Deutschland*. If, however, the local website of a given country has not yet been translated, it is wise to leave the country name in English; doing so indicates that the destination website is in English.

Shown below, Starbucks notes that the Austria website is in English and German. These details help users navigate to the right website the first time and have a better idea of what to expect when they arrive.

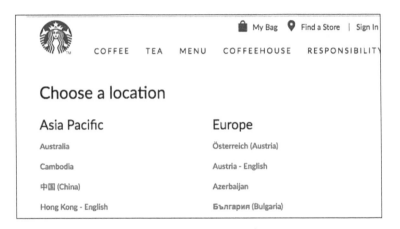

How to handle mixed-language websites

Few companies translate every word of their websites, which means that visitors are likely to click on a link that takes them away from their language back to English (or whatever is the default language).

First, linking to English content is okay. Users would rather have access to *all* available content on their localized websites even if some of that content is not yet translated.

But it's the manner in which you link to this non-translated content that can make the difference between a positive or negative experience.

There are two different solutions to this challenge:

Manage language experience with the links themselves

For links that take users to English-language content, add an icon or text to let users know the intended web page is not in his or her language. For example, here is how Autodesk Italy manages links that take the user back to English content.

Note the *inglese* text. Some CMS systems also allow for this text blurb to be automatically inserted and removed when the target content is eventually translated.

Better yet, leave some links untranslated

An alternative to adding *inglese* text is to simply decide *not* to translate any text link that will take users back to English content. By leaving these elements alone, it's instantly clear to the user that the content is not translated.

THINK OUTSIDE

*To give you a head start on going global,
here are insights into selected countries
and cultures.*

Think .cn

China

Everything seems bigger when thinking of China, and for good reason. The People's Republic of China (PRC) is the world's most populous country, with nearly 1.4 billion people. China is the world leader in internet users, with roughly 700 million. And China leads the world in travel, with more than 130 million outbound travelers per year.

According to the *Web Globalization Report Card*, Chinese is now effectively on par with English on global websites. In ten years it has grown from 65% to 97%.

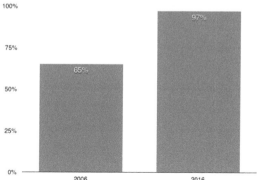

Chinese (Simplified) Usage on Global Websites

From mobile-first to mobile only

More than 120 million Chinese experience the internet through their smartphones and *only* their phones. And more than 80 percent of the sales on Singles Day are made through smartphones. Which means that your mobile website or app could make or break your success in this market.

Because Chinese are so phone-dependent, they will often use their phone numbers as their user names. Scannable QR codes are widely used because they allow for the rapid completion of a task, such as purchasing a product or ticket. Here's an example from China's leading rideshare company, Didi Chuxing:

It's worth noting that Uber recently invested in Didi, effectively ceding the market to this company. If a company as well financed and aggressive as Uber can't win in China, this should be a lesson to any Western company that views China as an "easy" win. China is anything but easy for Western companies to succeed in.

Here's another QR code example from Tmall, China's leading ecommerce platform (and originator of Singles Day):

You'll notice a number of familiar brands in this example; Western brands partner with Tmall the way they might partner with Amazon in the US. Costco, in fact, has no Chinese website and relies entirely on Tmall for its sales (shown here on Singles Day):

When you think Tmall, think Amazon—as its global ambitions are just as great.

Marriott in China

Marriott provides an excellent example of how an American-based company is going all out to win over Chinese travelers. In 2012, Marriott launched the Li Yu (礼遇) program, meaning *serving with courtesy*. The program caters to Chinese travelers with localized amenities, such as:

- Mandarin-speaking hotel associates.

- Complimentary Chinese tea and tea ware.

- TV and newspapers from China.

- Room numbers that include a 6 or 8 (considered lucky).

- Payment by AliPay.

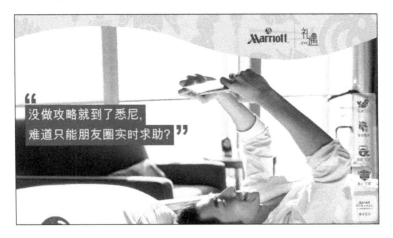

Marriott also now provides customer service via WeChat.

WeChat

Launched in 2011, WeChat is a mobile messaging app that has more than a billion users and has quickly moved beyond basic messaging. Users now link their bank accounts to the service and can purchase through WeChat. What about Facebook? In China the service is largely blocked by China's "great firewall," leaving services like WeChat free from Western competitors.

China's firewall incentivizes companies to host their websites within the country. But doing so requires a license that websites must display, and in-country representatives are legally responsible for all content displayed on the website, which can be a tricky proposition for some publishers. Apple hosts its website within China, as evidenced by the "ICP" license number in the footer of its website:

更多选购方式: 前往 Apple Store 零售店, 致电 400-666-8800 或查找在你附近的授权经销商。

Copyright © 2016 Apple Inc. 保留所有权利。   隐私政策 | 使用条款 | 销售政策 | 法律信息 | 网站

京公安网安备 11010502008968 京ICP备 10214630

Taiwan vs. mainland China

To most Chinese, Taiwan is not an independent country but a Chinese territory. Taiwan's leaders are quick to disagree and, in fact, the United Nations views Taiwan as an independent country.

But how do you present your company to both countries via your website without offending either party? You do so carefully. The first step is to avoid using the Taiwan flag on your website. I noted in *Think Visually* that companies should avoid using flags altogether, and this is one reason why.

Second, when you refer to the countries you support you should say "select your country/region" instead of just "select country."

Home	Africa	Available Languages			Available
Country/Regional Directory					
	Egypt	› English		South Africa	› English
	Kenya	› English			
	Asia				
	China	› 中文		Malaysia	› English
	Taiwan	› 臺灣		Pakistan	› English
	India	› English		Philippines	› English
	Indonesia	› Bahasa Indonesia › English		Singapore	› English

This type of semantic tightrope-walking is not ideal, but it does help you avoid incurring the wrath of millions of Chinese.

Simplified vs. Traditional Chinese

During China's Cultural Revolution, the Chinese language was "simplified" through a process of removing quite a few characters as well as removing strokes from characters that remained. The goal was to improve the literacy of the population by making the language easier to learn—a process that includes memorizing more than a thousand characters. Taiwan and Hong Kong, however, continue to use the traditional language. So if you want to reach Greater China via your website you'll need to support both written languages.

What about Mandarin? This is the spoken dialect used throughout much of mainland China. But you wouldn't say your website is displayed in Mandarin, rather in Simplified Chinese.

Hai tao

Shopping beyond borders is known as *hai tao*, which loosely translates into *ocean search*. According to *Internet Retailer*, more than 12 million Chinese purchased online from overseas merchants in 2012 in search of brand names, better prices, and higher-quality goods. For example, affluent Chinese parents will import diapers because of quality scares in years past with domestic brands. Imported nuts are also quite popular, as shown here on the Costco Tmall website:

The Kirkland brand is slowly but surely becoming a truly global brand.

Think .br

Brazil

Brazil is Latin America's largest economy but is still largely an emerging economy when it comes to ecommerce. Online sales are roughly $15 billion a year, compared to $400 billion in the US.

B2W Digital is Brazil's leading online retailer, managing a number of brands, such as the Latin American retailer Americanas:

Brazil has more than 140 million people with internet connections, but networks are slow compared to developed countries. Logistics remain a huge challenge; most roads are in poor condition, and the country lacks established carriers like FedEx or UPS. The national carrier Correios is notoriously slow.

Walmart has been investing heavily in the market over the past five years; the website is located at Walmart.com.br.

This is a screen shot from Black Friday, a major online shopping day in Brazil.

According to the *Web Globalization Report Card*, 91% of the leading global brands support localized websites for Brazil. Companies include:

- Adobe
- British Airways
- Hilton
- SAP

- Zara

Brazil vs. Brasil
Since Brazil is spelled *Brasil* in Portuguese, it makes good sense to use the native spelling to help web users find their local websites.

Portuguese (but not Portugal)
Portuguese is the official language of Brazil and should not be confused with the Portuguese spoken in Portugal. Although related, the languages sound quite different and use different vocabularies. The Portuguese alphabet includes 23 letters; the letters K, W, and Y are used in names and borrowed words. The language also makes heavy use of accented characters. The diacritic that often causes English speakers the most trouble is the cedilla (spelled *cedilha* in Portuguese), which, added to the c (ç) has the "S" sound.

Currency
The Brazilian currency is the Real (plural: Reais). The currency symbol is R$. International credit card penetration is still relatively low in the country, and customers are very sensitive to fraud; the most popular domestic credit card is Elo, carried by roughly 50 million customers. Amazon in Brazil supports payment by Elo.

About 30% of all online transactions in Brazil are through a system known as Boleto Bancário, which is similar to a "pro forma" invoice. The customer receives a bar code bank slip as an invoice and then pays for it at a local bank in cash, which can even be used for completing online transactions.

Boleto (which means *ticket*) is not well suited for recurring transactions, and Netflix struggled when it first entered Brazil in part because it did not offer flexible payment options. As shown here, Netflix now offers support for Elo, debit cards, and direct debit:

Lucky numbers

As in the US, 13 is an unlucky number to most Brazilians. But it is also viewed by many to be a lucky number. Friday the 13th is, however, widely viewed as an ominous day. The number 7 is considered by many to be a lucky number.

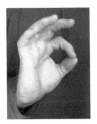

Gestures

Beware of the OK hand sign. The OK sign that Americans often use may be considered offensive in Brazil and other countries. That's because it appears closely related to the offensive gesture shown below:

As an alternative, use the thumbs-up gesture, which is as positive in Brazil as it is in the US.

Colors

The yellow in the Brazilian flag symbolizes the country's wealth in gold, the green signifies Brazil's lush natural landscape, and the blue signifies the sky. The colors of the Brazilian flag are not only seen as positive colors, they are seen on everything—clothing, uniforms, signage, and corporate logos, such as Localiza.

White is also a positive color and a sign of good fortune. On New Year's Eve, people may dress in white clothing in reference to the African goddess of the sea, Iemenjá. On this date, Brazilians will toss white flowers into the sea to please Iemenjá and hope for a good year. As with all colors, there are exceptions to the rule; the popular Brazilian beer Brahma is easily recognized by its red and white logo.

Think .de

Germany

The largest European economy and third-largest economy overall, Germany is considered a core market for most large multinationals. Not surprisingly, according to the *Web Globalization Report Card*, 95% of the leading global brands support German-language websites. Companies include:

- American Express
- Canon
- Gucci
- MasterCard
- Pepsi
- Under Armour

Privacy matters

Consumer privacy is of huge importance to Germans, and the country (as well as the EU) has some of the strictest consumer protection laws around. In the aftermath of the Edward Snowden release of NSA documents, German courts ruled that American companies could no longer transmit German consumer data out of the country. In 2016, it fined Adobe, Pepsi, and Unilever for doing just that. Companies that want to do business in Germany need to have a plan for legally managing consumer information, as well as staying on top of the fast-evolving privacy landscape.

Germans and credit cards

While Germans are very comfortable shopping online, they are not very comfortable using credit cards. They prefer to pay by bank transfer or by eWallet, such as PayPal. Netflix has localized its website for Germany so that customers can pay by direct debit, as shown here:

Don't repeat Walmart's mistakes

Walmart entered Germany in 1998 and spent hundreds of millions of dollars opening stores across the country only to give up and withdraw in 2006. Here is the home page from the since-abandoned website:

Culturally, Walmart ran into problems trying to force employees to adopt the cultural practices of its American employees, such as the morning group chant and smiling at customers. Germans find excessive smiling either rude or untrustworthy. But even after Walmart adapted to the culture they suffered from their anti-union approach to labor and store locations that were in less desirable locations. Even after opening more than 80 stores, the company failed. One of the essential questions companies must ask before trying to go global is *How world-ready is our company culture?* And where can we evolve our culture to adapt to local markets without sacrificing who we are? If Walmart had posed these questions it might not have struggled so.

Think .in

India

The Republic of India, with a population of 1.2 billion, ranks only second in population to China. The country is also the seventh-largest country by area.

Think beyond big numbers

Yes, India has more than a billion residents, yet only 400 million have internet access, primarily through their phones. And millions of these mobile users are on slower 3G networks. In addition, buying power is limited and credit card usage quite low. India's poor infrastructure, much like Brazil, makes distribution particularly challenging. Nevertheless, the country is one of the fastest growing ecommerce markets as millions of people become more comfortable shopping online.

Think beyond English

If you spend time visiting websites localized for India, you might assume that your website need only support English, since most websites do just this. But the fact is that India is home to more than 20 official languages. Here are the top seven languages ranked by number of native speakers:

Hindi	422 million
Bengali	83 million
Telugu	75 million
Tamil	61 million
Urdu	52 million
Gujurati	46 million
Malayalam	33 million

As a point of comparison, there are 80 million native speakers of French and 65 million native speakers of Italian.

English rules, for now

According to the *Web Globalization Report Card*, only Hindi has surpassed 5% penetration.

Companies that support one or more Indian languages include:

- BBC
- Facebook
- Google
- Microsoft
- Twitter
- Uber

YouTube, as shown on its global gateway menu on the following page, supports an impressive 10 Indian languages.

Amazon vs. Flipkart

Amazon, having lost out to Alibaba in China (for now), is investing heavily in India. It now has more than 20 distribution centers across the country and offers its Prime membership service for roughly $15 per year. The company claims that during the 2016 Diwali festival (the major ecommerce holiday) it sold 15 million units, compared with Flipkart's 15.5 million units.

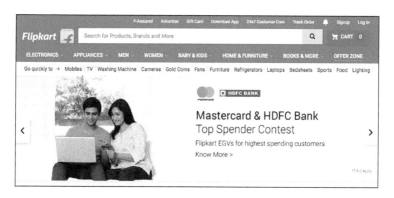

Nevertheless, home-grown Flipkart, along with Snapdeal, remain the leading ecommerce companies, accounting for more than half of all online sales.

Localized menus

India is home to approximately 500 million vegetarians based on a widespread belief in *Ahimsa*, the Buddhist term for doing no harm. As a result, Western restaurant chains such as McDonald's have had to significantly localize their menus to appeal to the market. Shown below is the vegetarian McAloo burger:

Cows are revered in many parts of India and, in fact, are protected by law. The way animals are depicted in advertisements is just as important as the depiction of people.

All that glitters

It's impossible to convey the importance that gold holds over the majority of the country. India is one of the world's major importers of gold. Because only a third of Indians have bank accounts, gold is viewed as the best place to keep one's money. Gold also fuels a hidden banking system in which money is transferred without taxes or any government tracking.

Gold is the customary gift for weddings, celebrations, and Diwali. Here is a sample page from Amazon India's home page, promoting the holiday of lights:

Think .th

Thailand

Home to 68 million people, Thailand is the world's 20th-most-populous country. The official language is Thai, and the script looks like this:

According to the *Web Globalization Report Card*, Thai is now seen on 55% of the websites studied, up from 30% in 2001. Among the websites that now support Thai are:

- Air France
- Coca-Cola

- Ford
- IKEA
- John Deere
- Kayak
- PayPal
- Twitter
- Visa

Web localization: as simple as black and white

The death of Thailand's King Bhumibol Adulyadej in 2016 led to stores running out of black and white clothing as the population mourned its leader in color-appropriate clothing.

What did this mean for website localization? Consider the following Thailand websites, starting with Apple:

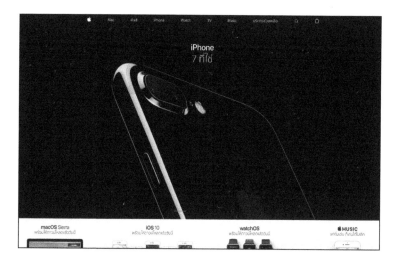

Samsung:

Nike:

Starbucks:

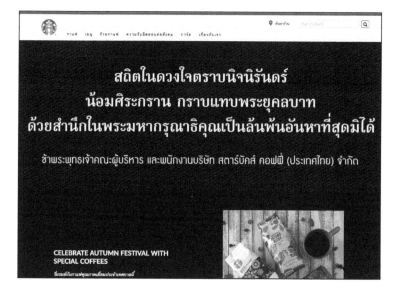

Web localization isn't about launching a localized website and forgetting about it. It's about creating a living and breathing website that responds quickly to local events, as these companies did.

Think .uk

United Kingdom

The United Kingdom of Great Britain and Northern Ireland includes four countries: England, Wales, Scotland, and Northern Ireland. The definition of *united* is under some duress as a result of the 2016 Brexit vote. While England voted to exit the European Union, many in Scotland and Northern Ireland have threatened to leave the UK if this comes to pass.

Separated by a common language

A quote attributed to both Oscar Wilde and Winston Churchill: *England and America are two countries separated by a common language.*

For many years, most US companies resisted translating their American English websites into British English. After all, English speakers on both sides of the pond can muddle through each other's respective languages, but neither language will appear *local*.

Most companies have since realized that if they truly want to be perceived as local, even English requires a bit of translation. According to the *Web Globalization Report Card*, 77 percent of the leading global websites now translate into British English.

When is a rental car not a rental car?

In the UK, *rental cars* don't exist. But *car hires* do. So if you're Enterprise you adapt. As shown here:

Terminology may seem trivial at first, but imagine the complexity that retailers face when selling in the UK. Shown below, Amazon must work with a very distinct index of terms.

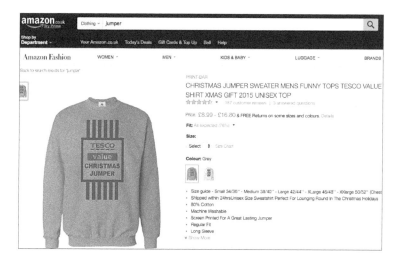

Sweaters become *jumpers*, *running shoes* become *trainers*, *strollers* become *prams*.

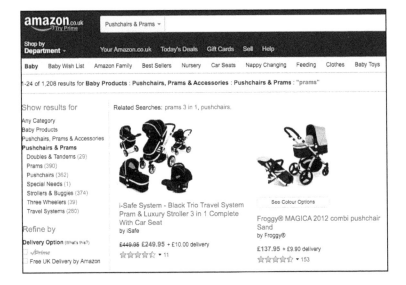

This is not an English-only challenge.

Spanish also varies by country. And while many companies successfully translate into a *universal* Spanish that bridges many countries, their ultimate trajectory will be to support distinct flavors of Spanish for each market.

Think .au

Australia

If you're in search of wide-open spaces, look no further than Australia. In this country a population of 24 million (fewer than California) occupies a land area similar to the continental US. But if you want to find most Australians, you don't have to look very far. More than 80% of the population lives within 50 miles of the coast, most within the major cities of Sydney, Melbourne, Brisbane, Perth, and Adelaide.

Australian English

When translating for Australia, most international companies reuse their British translations, which is fine, to a point. Australia does share in British spellings such as *colour* and *analyse*. But Australians have also developed a unique vocabulary of words such as:

- arvo (afternoon)
- doco (documentary)
- rellies (relatives)
- sanger (sandwich)
- servo (gas station)

If you want your Australian content to appear truly local, hire an Australian translator to take a final pass at your content before going live with it.

Catch of the Day vs. Amazon

While Australians are well aware of Amazon, they are more enamored of the ecommerce conglomerate Catch of the Day.

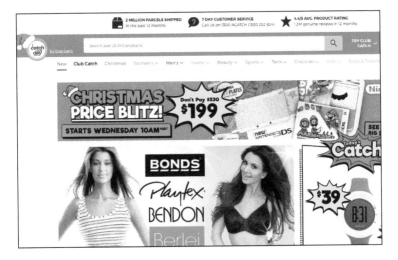

This home-grown ecommerce company consists of several brands and is the largest online retailer in Australia. Its Club Catch membership program offers free shipping and boasts more than four million members.

Switching seasons

When most Americans are wearing winter coats, Australians are at the beach. And this difference in seasons poses both challenges and opportunities to non-Australian companies. Savvy clothing retailers can now market winter and beach clothing year round by serving customers on both sides of the equator.

Target vs. Target

Target is a major retailer in Australia. But the Target in Australia is completely unrelated to the North American company. Shown here is the Target Australia home page:

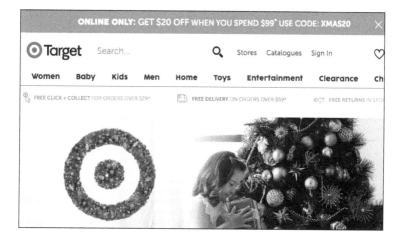

It's only a matter of time before the two Targets, as they pursue global expansion, come to terms with their conflicting brands. And this underscores a larger issue about the globalization of brands—*when going global, the world is surprisingly small*. It's not uncommon to see would-be global brands replicated (intentionally or unintentionally) by in-country equivalents.

Think .ru

Russia

Russia is the second-largest economy in Europe, the eighth most populous country in the world, and is the destination of an increasing number of multinational companies. According to the *Web Globalization Report Card*, 88% of the leading global brands support localized websites for Russia, including Nike, shown here:

Other companies that offer Russian-language websites include:

- Apple

- Delta

- FedEx

- IKEA

- Starbucks

- Visa

But succeeding in Russia isn't easy. The Russian language poses unique branding and localization challenges, and internet penetration is still largely an urban phenomenon.

Country size

At more than 17 million square kilometers, Russia is the largest country in the world. It is nearly twice the size of the United States. Russia consists of 26 states and 1 federal district—spanning 11 time zones. With a country so large and infrastructure still developing, product fulfillment is one of the major challenges that companies face here.

Locals rule

In Russia, local upstarts have given US tech companies a tough fight. For example, the leading search engine is Yandex (<u>Yandex.ru</u>) which, like its US-based competitor Google, offers a host of services including email, maps, and shopping. Russia, unlike China, does not block Google within Russia. So Yandex had to succeed on its own merits, which it credits to simply having a better understanding of Russian consumers and the language itself. Shown below is the Yandex home page:

The leading social platform is VKontakte (VK.ru), which looks not unlike Facebook:

Currency

The ruble (also spelled *rouble*) is the currency of Russia and Belarus and several other post-Soviet countries. One ruble is divided into 100 kopeks (or *copecks*). For years there was no official symbol for the ruble; it was typically displayed as руб until 2013, when an official symbol for the ruble was launched:

Russians prefer to pay by eWallet services, namely Yandex Money (money.yandex.com), which now supports Apple Pay, and Webmoney (www.webmoney.com). PayPal still has relatively low penetration in Russia, and credit cards have been slow to take off.

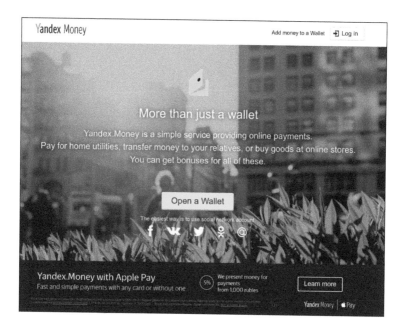

The Russian language

Russian is the primary language of roughly 150 million people. It is the official language of Russia, Belarus, Kazakhstan, and Kyrgyzstan, and is one of the six official languages of the United Nations. Russian is a Slavic language and is closely related to Ukrainian and Belarusian.

Russian is one of the more challenging languages for native-English speakers to learn, not just because of the Cyrillic characters, but because nouns can be spelled in a bewildering variety of ways depending on usage.

The Romanization of Russian

The process of converting Cyrillic characters into Latin characters is known as transliteration. For example, Russian search portal Yandex is a transliteration of Яндекс. Western companies often transliterate their brand names into Cyrillic characters when entering the market.

The most common mistake companies make when transliterating their brand names is the failure to test the names for possible double entendres. One famous example is the instant noodle brand Dosirak. The name, when pronounced according to the transliterated spelling, sounded similar to a vulgar Russian word. This misunderstanding was such a problem that the brand name was eventually changed from Dosirak to Doshirak.

Same word, different endings

Another typical mistake made by virtually all companies without a Slavic background is the failure to understand that Russian is a highly flexible language in which the declension of proper names, including company names and trademarks, is subject to up to nine cases. In other words, the ending syllables of your company name and the names of your products will change. They will be pronounced differently in different situations, depending on the grammatical case. In Russian, you're not drinking Coca-Cola, you're drinking Coca-Colu; you're not running out of Coca-Cola, but rather out of Coca-Coly; your life is not better with Coca-Cola, but with Coca-Coloy.

Companies often deal with this complexity by choosing not to deal with it at all. They will use one case exclusively—typically the nominative case—regardless of how odd it may sound to Russians. Ideally, a company will be more flexible with how its brand name is used, making it appear much more local than its foreign counterparts.

Be patient with interpreters

It can take up to 10% longer to say something in Russian than in English. Russian translators say that it may require up to four Russian words to convey the meaning of one English word. And some English words and phrases simply have no Russian equivalent, such as *privacy, efficiency*, and *take care*.

Negatives

The Russian language makes liberal use of negatives, and a positive idea is often expressed using negatives. To say something is "big," a Russian might say it "is not small." Given that Americans make liberal use of positive language, one can see how literal translations may come across as "foreign" to a Russian reader.

Check your coat at the door

It is considered *nyekulturno* (bad manners) not to check your coat at the entrance of an office building, restaurant, or other public building. Others types of *nyekulturno* include:

- Standing with your hands in your pockets.

- Sprawling in your chair.

- Resting your arm over the back of a chair.

- Crossing your legs so as to show the sole of your shoe.

- Crossing your arms behind your head.

- Sitting with legs spread wide.

Be careful that any photos of people you use on your website do not exhibit *nyekulturno*.

Positive colors

The colors of the Russian flag are widely perceived to be positive colors. The flag itself dates back to Peter the Great, and there is no official meaning associated with the three colors. One popular theory is that white represents God, blue represents the tsar, and red represents the people. Others say that white represents the heavens, blue represents the sky, and red is the earth.

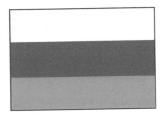

Bolsheviks carried a red flag when they overthrew the tsar, and red has since been synonymous with communism. However, despite the failure of communism, red still carries a very positive message and is found in many of the more recently created corporate logos.

Negative colors

Black is both a positive and negative color. Everything depends upon context, as black is associated with funerals. The colors brown and gray, though not considered to be purely negative, are not viewed as positive colors. Giving yellow flowers to a woman may be perceived as a sign of bad luck or a sign of the end of the affair.

Positive gestures

- The thumbs-up sign.

- The OK sign is a positive sign to Russians who recognize it; however, many Russians do not recognize this gesture.

Negative gestures

- Pointing your finger at someone.

- The thumbs-down sign.

- Tapping one's forehead (quite rude), or, more commonly, putting one's index finger onto one's temple and quickly turning it a few times back and forth.

Odd-numbered flowers

Never give a Russian an even number of flowers. Even numbers are for the dead. Always give odd numbers. When you order a dozen or two dozen roses, ask for an extra flower for good luck.

Beware the threshold
Do not shake hands or kiss over the threshold of a door. Russians believe doing so allows evil spirits to enter the home. Also, do not whistle in the house or in a car as some believe you are "whistling your money away."

Married?
Russians wear their wedding rings on the right ring finger, not the left.

Think .ar

Arabic

While the country code .ar refers to Argentina, .ar is also a language code, which refers to Arabic. Languages also have codes, most of them in two digits, such as .en for English and .ro for Romanian. Arabic is one of the world's major languages, with 420 million speakers across more than 22 countries. And Arabic is also one of the few bidirectional languages in the world, along with Persian and Urdu. Notice here on the Adobe website how Arabic text is displayed from right to left but Latin text remains as is.

Arabic can be an intimidating and technically challenging language to support, but more and more companies are making the investment. According to the *Web Globalization Report Card*, 53% of the leading global brands now support Arabic.

The regional approach to Arabic

Because Arabic covers such a wide geographic reach, companies often begin their localization efforts by creating a Middle Eastern regional website in Arabic. While spoken Arabic varies greatly across this region, written Arabic is mostly consistent.

Here is the NIVEA Middle East home page.

I've included the US home page as well so you can see how the design "flips" when it is localized into Arabic.

Samsung also flips its web design on its Arabic-language site:

When thinking ecommerce, think locally

While a regional approach is a sound first step, if you want to support ecommerce, you'll need to think locally. Middle Eastern payment processor Payfort publishes a state-of-the-industry report every year. In 2016, it released data on the leading countries based on internet users.

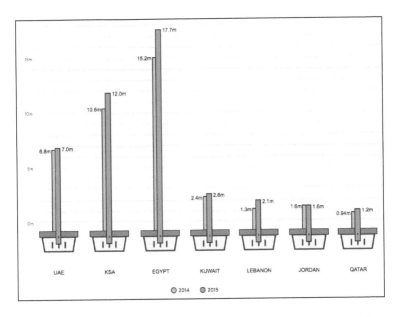

As you can see, Egypt dominates the rest of the region in number of shoppers. But Egyptians don't have a high rate of credit card usage, which creates other challenges.

Kuwait has a small online population but one with high credit card penetration.

The leading ecommerce company in the region is Souq.com, shown here:

Notice the logo positioned on the right side of the header with the search engine and cart on the left side—the opposite of, say, Amazon.com.

And think young

Throughout much of the Middle East, the young outnumber the old and are forcing changes in culture and technology. For example, in Saudi Arabia more than 70 percent of the population is under 30 years of age.

BECOMING WORLD-READY

A few final thoughts about thriving in a smaller world.

We are more alike than we are different

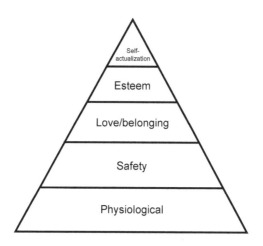

While most of this book is devoted to the many ways that we differ from one another around the world, I maintain that these differences are far outweighed by similarities.

When it comes to going global, you don't have to look much further than the many country websites of Amazon to see more similarities than differences.

Such as on the home pages for India and France:

The clothing is different, the holidays are different, the prices and product mix are different. But the fundamental web design remains the same.

And consider Facebook, which supports nearly two billion users through a service that is largely consistent around the world. Here is Facebook's global gateway in all 98 languages:

Select Your Language

Suggested Languages	English (US) ✓	Español	Português (Brasil)	Français (France)
All Languages	Af-Soomaali	Gaeilge	Shqip	□□□□□□□□
Africa and Middle East	Afrikaans	Galego	Ślōnskŏ gŏdka	नेपाली
Americas	Azərbaycan dili	Guarani	Slovenčina	मराठी
Asia-Pacific	Bahasa Indonesia	Hausa	Slovenščina	हिन्दी
Eastern Europe	Bahasa Melayu	Hrvatski	Suomi	অসমীয়া
Western Europe	Basa Jawa	Ikinyarwanda	Svenska	বাংলা
	Bisaya	Íslenska	Tiếng Việt	ਪੰਜਾਬੀ
	Bosanski	Italiano	Türkçe	ગુજરાતી
	Brezhoneg	Kiswahili	Ελληνικά	ଓଡ଼ିଆ
	Català	Kurdî (Kurmancî)	Беларуская	தமிழ்
	Čeština	Latviešu	Български	తెలుగు
	Corsu	Lietuvių	Қазақша	ಕನ್ನಡ
	Cymraeg	Magyar	Македонски	മലയാളം
	Dansk	Malagasy	Монгол	සිංහල
	Deutsch	Malti	Русский	ภาษาไทย
	Eesti	Nederlands	Српски	မြန်မာဘာသာ
	English (UK)	Nederlands (België)	Точикӣ	ភាសាខ្មែរ
	English (US)	Norsk (bokmål)	Українська	한국어
	Español	Norsk (nynorsk)	ქართული	中文(台灣)
	Español (España)	O'zbek	اردو	中文(简体)
	Euskara	Polski	עברית	中文(香港)
	Filipino	Português (Brasil)	اردو	日本語
	Føroyskt	Português (Portugal)	العربية	日本語(関西)
	Français (Canada)	Pulaar	پښتو	
	Français (France)	Română	فارسی	

So why are we so sensitive to websites that aren't well localized for our cultures? Perhaps because we are sensitive to what makes us unique. Perhaps one of Maslow's unwritten needs is the need to feel special, as in a member of a tribe. And part of feeling special requires acknowledging the differences between one another. But in the greater scheme, these differences are quite minimal. Maslow's Hierarchy of Needs isn't unique to one culture or country. We all share the need for food and shelter and, ultimately, love.

We're all translators

You don't need "translator" in your job title to find yourself translating. If you're a software developer you spend your days translating technology to your marketing team. If you're a marketer you translate new social trends to your product team. No matter where you look within a company, translation is happening all around you.

And when you get home you continue your role as translator. We translate to our partners, our children. Our children translate to us.

Why does this matter?

Because it's important to understand that translation is not some specialized service that you only rely on when you want to expand into a new country. Translation isn't limited to languages. Translation is a part our lives. And as the world becomes smaller, translation is something we could all stand to become better at.

The rise of the translator class
Translating is an art form, and translators are artists, like writers. They have creative mindsets, which generally leads to a group of very strong-willed, outspoken people. These people are the first

to tell you that your new brand name won't fly in, say, Japan.

Translators are empathetic by design. They *have* to understand how their readers will perceive the translated text or video or software interface. And the best translators can communicate this intelligence back up the corporate ladder.

The problem is that we don't always want bad news. Our naming agency tells us that the new brand name is perfect. Our lawyers say that we can get the trademark in all the countries we have eyes on. And then along comes a translator from Japan who says our brand name is all wrong for her country.

But translators can be your secret weapon in going global. They are user advocates, they provide input into product design and naming, and they are co-creators in their own right.

The translator class includes those who translate ideas, images, cultures, and concepts. The translator class is responsible for helping companies expand into new markets around the world. And, as we all become better global generalists, we too become part of this emerging translator class.

Globalization is a journey, not a destination

This is a true story

The marketing director of a professional membership society wanted to expand its subscriber base in other countries. The society already had a good number of international members but because none of the publications had been translated, members needed at least a moderate grasp of English to reap the benefits of joining.

The marketing director decided to translate the society's membership form into Chinese in the hopes that it would make the process of joining much easier for Chinese speakers and increase membership. The membership form was translated by in-country volunteers, and within a few weeks the society received its first completed form by fax.

The membership director, who was unaware of what the marketing director had been up to, looked at this form, filled out in Chinese, and said, "What the hell am I supposed to do with this?"

The membership director didn't understand Chinese. No one on her staff understood Chinese. Even if someone on her staff did understand Chinese, their membership database didn't accept Chinese characters.

So this person in China completed the membership form and subscribed to a couple of publications—and the organization could do nothing about it. They didn't even know what publications were selected because the publication names were translated into Chinese—and they had no English-language template to compare it against.

The perils of premature globalization

It may seem obvious not to create marketing materials in a language that your company can't support, yet this scenario is frequently repeated by companies that leap into global markets prematurely. Before your company takes that fateful leap, make sure that you can not only support a global website, but can support the issues that arise once that website goes live.

Launching a global website does not necessarily make a company any more globally aware. Localization vendors can do all the heavy lifting and have your new local website ready to go in a matter of weeks. But are you ready for what comes after? The texts, emails, and phone calls in different languages? Questions about shipping, returns, and refunds?

When you consider just how much work you invest in your domestic website—creating new content, fixing bugs, adapting to new technologies and social trends—it's safe to assume that you may invest just as much effort on developing and maintaining each local website or app.

Going global is a state of mind

Globalization isn't as much about being global as it is about *thinking* globally. Between wanting to go global and actually going global lies a great stretch of failed websites, wasted money, and lost jobs. Everyone wants to sell their products and services in as many places as possible. But it's the actual process of getting into each country that proves to be the bridge too far for many companies.

So it's important that you and your team—particularly your executives—have a clear idea of the challenges and costs involved. Going global is a journey, and there are bumps in the road.

Just as your English-language website opened a new world of opportunities domestically, so too will each localized website. But localization will only succeed if your entire organization supports it, from the executive suite to the factory floor to the customer support line.

Globalization requires keeping an open mind toward foreign languages, cultures, and traditions. Never assume what works in one country will work everywhere else. And be prepared to take your treasured brands and products and rename them, reposition them, or scrap them altogether when entering a new market.

Your entire organization should place a priority on understanding foreign cultures. If we have indeed entered a knowledge economy, those employees and those companies that are most "globally aware" will be best prepared to succeed.

Enjoy the journey

When I was first tasked with localizing a website, back when few websites were in any other language than English, I remembered the excitement I felt in working with translators who knew the languages. I made mistakes along the way. So many mistakes. But I also learned my way around languages like Japanese and Arabic and German. I learned how to avoid mistakes that other companies were making. And I enjoyed the journey.

It's my hope that this book gives you a head start on your journey. I encourage you to stay in touch with me at my blog Global by Design (www.globalbydesign.com) and by the newsletter that I send out through the website. As you encounter questions or learn something worth sharing, please let me know.

John Yunker

jyunker@bytelevel.com

RESOURCES

*Here are a few additional resources to
assist you on your global journey.*

The ultimate globalization checklist

While this list is by no means definitive and is geared in large part to the globalization of websites and software, it does cover many of the key issues companies face when taking any product or service global. Share it with your marketing, web, and IT teams before you launch your next globalization project.

Planning

- Where do you want to go?
  - ° Identify your target markets and locales.
  - ° Evaluate your products and services from the eyes of target users. Is there demand and, if so, what localization will be required of your products?
  - ° Do you have visitor logs that show who is visiting your website and from where? What users are self-translating your website—and into which languages?

- Evaluate the world readiness of your brand.
  - ° Test the effectiveness of your company and brand names in these new markets, or create new ones.
  - ° For websites, register country-code domain names.

- Assess your company's global readiness.
  - High-level executive commitment is required.
  - Have you budgeted not only for initial localization but also for ongoing maintenance of content?
  - Do your teams understand the process of globalization?
  - Are in-country offices engaged and ready to implement, review, and support localized websites and social networking?
- Infrastructure planning
  - Will you host your local websites in the target markets?
- Customer support
  - How will you manage non-English customer support phone calls and emails?
  - How do you handle returns and refunds?
  - Do delivery schedules take into account local holidays?
- Metrics and KPIs
  - What metrics will you use to measure success (i.e., leads and/or sales generated)?
- Global ecommerce
  - How will you manage currency, rates, processing?
  - Is the user aware of how currency will be charged on credit card?
  - How will you mitigate fraud?

Internationalization

- Develop global design templates.
  - Flexible layouts, to allow for 100% text expansion in headers and up to 50% in body text. For example, German text will expand an additional 40% on average.
  - Remove embedded text from visuals whenever possible. Instead rely on CSS to position text over images.
  - Remove extraneous visuals. The remaining visuals should be culturally neutral.
  - Are icons globally user friendly?
  - Leave extra room for external plugins (Facebook social, for example) which may expand considerably.
  - Multiple templates may be designed, for example, for "full featured" local sites vs. lightweight "brochure" sites.
  - If you provide web pages and/or documents to be printed by the user, will they adapt to local paper size conventions?
  - Local offices should be involved to ensure their needs are met.

- Develop flexibility to support market-specific business logic, promotional elements, and content on a per-market basis. For example:
  - Seasonality. Some sites may promote summer destinations while other sites may promote winter destinations.
  - Legal limitations. Some markets may not allow travel to certain countries.

- Business limitations. Some cultures may value different amenities more than others, forcing a reconfiguration of amenity lists and featured images.

- Technical web/software requirements:
  - For your website and software, separate style settings from code via language-specific CSS files.
  - Add an extra point for Asian scripts to improve legibility.
  - Provide developers with guidelines for handling text expansion for buttons and legibility for Asian scripts.
  - Avoid specifying font faces unless you plan for extensive client-side testing.
  - Extract text strings from code. Create world-ready software that pulls text from resource files based on specific locale/culture settings.
  - Avoid programmatically generated text when possible. Use complete sentences, including punctuation, to send to translators.
  - Look closely for hidden text strings, such as error messages.
  - If you have sorted lists in your application (i.e., glossary or index), how will this change as your target language changes?

- Develop support for local date/time formats, measurements, currency, mailing, and other region-specific features and content.
  - Leverage existing locale/culture libraries when possible, such as CLDR and Globalize.js.
  - For example, some users may think 2/10/2010 means October 2nd, while others may think February 10th.

Best to display the data as February 10, 2010.

- If user data is collected via ecommerce and other transactions, separate databases may be required.

- Test stability and flexibility of websites/software by inserting different languages/scripts (a process known as pseudo-localization). Look for clipped text strings.

- Analyze existing visuals for global relevance: Colors, icons, symbols, promotional elements.
    - Avoid any visuals that may risk offending users.

- Photos of people are typically the most risky. Clothing, ethnicity, and gestures may result in unintended consequences.

- Collateral: Are downloadable brochures in the proper size for the market, such as A4 for UK?

- Content globalization
    - Is the source text ready for translation (i.e., free of humor, slang, Americanisms)? Note that translators can effectively work around such issues, but removing them at the start makes for faster workflow.
    - Do you have all text strings identified and isolated? For example, text strings may be scattered about in software application code instead of extracted into resource files.
    - Develop a terminology glossary. These terms should be widely agreed upon and shared with all content creators to ensure consistency in source content and also consistent translation.
    - Determine the best content workflow based on in-country people/vendors, tools, and needs.

- Develop a global gateway strategy:
  - Include a permanent global gateway in the top right corner of every web page of your site. This allows the web user to easily change settings no matter where he or she lands.
  - The global gateway should include a globe icon to convey meaning across all languages.
  - Avoid using flags, and never use flags to indicate language. Display languages and country/region names in their native languages (i.e., *Deutsch* rather than *German*).
  - Don't play favorites. For example, do not put United States or United Kingdom at the top of a country pull-down menu.
  - For mobile apps, align the language with the operating system language. But also give users the ability to change language setting.

- Have you planned for local data privacy regulations and taxes?

- How will you manage user expectations if the localized website does not include all the same features and products as the source website?

Localization
- Define the scope of your project, including the number of words and images requiring localization.
  - Think "scenario-based" localization, in which you focus on key usage scenarios, such as ecommerce, production information, and sales lead queries.

- SEO should play a role in translation of not only

keywords but also buzzwords, slang, etc.

- ° Is your search engine optimized for local terminology? For example, "jumpers" in the UK vs. "sweaters" in the US.

- Estimate and allocate your budget. Set the schedule.
  - ° Develop your agency RFP.
  - ° Select your Language Service Provider (LSP).
  - ° Prepare your source files, such as text, graphics, and scripts. Prepare detailed instructions for the translators.
  - ° Develop translation style guide, which includes notes for translators on terminology, audience, tone, and cultural sensitivity.
  - ° Different types of source text will require different types of translation (and possibly different translators). Legal text will need to be faithfully translated while marketing text may be "transcreated."

- Is translated text being stored in a translation memory for future reuse?
  - ° Always be sure that you own (in writing) your translation memories when you work with a translation vendor.

- Begin localization:
  - ° Translation
  - ° Editing
  - ° Graphics and design localization (if required)
  - ° In-country reviews (by staff and/or vendor)

Maintenance and Customer Support

- Train in-country staff to support content and customers.

- Localization maintenance:
  - New source content must be localized.
  - New keywords must be managed across languages.
  - Changes to existing content must be reflected on all localized sites.
  - Support customers via all channels, including phone, email, and in-store.
  - Promote localized sites with advertising, PR, and search (SEO/SEM) initiatives.

- Translation re-use via translation memory tools.

Measurement and Improvement

- Analyze web traffic, leads, and sales by market.

- Conduct quality audits of the translation(s).

A few global resources

Every day I have more questions than I have answers. Which is why I spend a lot of my time on other websites and news outlets. I'm assuming you're already keeping an eye on *The Economist*, *Bloomberg*, and the *BBC*. Here are some additional resources that I recommend:

Country Data
CIA World Factbook:
www.cia.gov/library/publications/the-world-factbook

Ecommerce Insights
Internet Retailer: www.internetretailer.com

PYMTS: www.pymnts.com

Tech in Asia: www.techinasia.com

Globalization News/Resources
Multilingual: www.multilingual.com

globalEDGE at Michigan State University: globaledge.msu.

edu

Globalization & Localization Association: www.gala-global.org

Global Small Business Blog: www.globalsmallbusinessblog.com

Training
The Localization Institute: www.localizationinstitute.com

UW Localization Certificate: www.pce.uw.edu

Web Globalization Best Practices
Global by Design: www.globalbydesign.com

World Wide Web Consortium Internationalization Activity: www.w3.org/International

Unicode Common Locale Data Repository: http://cldr.unicode.org

Acknowledgments

It's impossible to thank everyone who has broadened my world over the years and directly and indirectly contributed to this book. But you know who you are, and I am grateful for all your patiently answered questions.

For the *think .ru* chapter I wish to thank Ala Maleika, Alex Evstyugov-Babaev, Alexey Smirnov, Anna Pigalova, Elena S.McGivern, and Valery Legotin for their contributions. For the *think .br* chapter I wish to thank Teddy Bengtsson, Fabiano Cid, Aleksander França Honma, and Liam Gallagher for their contributions.

And, most important, thanks to Midge Raymond for her invaluable input every step along the way.

About the author

Co-founder of Byte Level Research (www.bytelevel.com), John has helped hundreds of companies and organizations improve their global websites and marketing efforts. He wrote the first book devoted to the emerging field of web globalization, *Beyond Borders: Web Globalization Strategies* and has written a number of landmark reports, including 13 annual editions of *The Web Globalization Report Card*. John is a regular speaker at industry events such as Unicode Conference, Internet Retailer, and Localization World. He has a bachelor's degree from the University of Missouri School of Journalism and an MS from Boston University. He blogs at www.GlobalbyDesign.com.

About the publisher

Byte Level Books is dedicated to helping individuals and companies succeed locally and globally. A division of Byte Level Research, we publish books for marketers, developers, and athletes. To learn more, visit us at www.bytelevelbooks.com.

CPSIA information can be obtained
at www.ICGtesting.com
Printed in the USA
FSHW01n2051200218
44554FS

9 781618 220493